ROUTLEDGE LIBRARY EDITIONS: LIBRARY AND INFORMATION SCIENCE

Volume 75

REFERENCE SERVICES AND TECHNICAL SERVICES

REFERENCE SERVICES AND TECHNICAL SERVICES
Interactions in Library Practice

Edited by
GORDON STEVENSON AND
SALLY STEVENSON

Routledge
Taylor & Francis Group
LONDON AND NEW YORK

First published in 1984 by The Haworth Press, Inc.

This edition first published in 2020
by Routledge
2 Park Square, Milton Park, Abingdon, Oxon OX14 4RN

and by Routledge
52 Vanderbilt Avenue, New York, NY 10017

Routledge is an imprint of the Taylor & Francis Group, an informa business

© 1984 The Haworth Press, Inc.

All rights reserved. No part of this book may be reprinted or reproduced or utilised in any form or by any electronic, mechanical, or other means, now known or hereafter invented, including photocopying and recording, or in any information storage or retrieval system, without permission in writing from the publishers.

Trademark notice: Product or corporate names may be trademarks or registered trademarks, and are used only for identification and explanation without intent to infringe.

British Library Cataloguing in Publication Data
A catalogue record for this book is available from the British Library

ISBN: 978-0-367-34616-4 (Set)
ISBN: 978-0-429-34352-0 (Set) (ebk)
ISBN: 978-0-367-40658-5 (Volume 75) (hbk)
ISBN: 978-0-367-40660-8 (Volume 75) (pbk)
ISBN: 978-0-367-80830-3 (Volume 75) (ebk)

Publisher's Note
The publisher has gone to great lengths to ensure the quality of this reprint but points out that some imperfections in the original copies may be apparent.

Disclaimer
The publisher has made every effort to trace copyright holders and would welcome correspondence from those they have been unable to trace.

Reference Services and Technical Services: Interactions in Library Practice

Edited by
Gordon Stevenson and Sally Stevenson

The Haworth Press
New York

Reference Services and Technical Services: Interactions in Library Practice has also been published as *The Reference Librarian*, Number 9, Fall/Winter 1983.

Copyright © 1984 by The Haworth Press, Inc. All rights reserved. Copies of articles in this publication may be noncommercially reproduced for the purpose of educational advancement. Otherwise, no part of this work may be reproduced or utilized in any form or by any means, electronic or mechanical, including photocopying, microfilm, and recording, or by any information storage and retrieval system, without permission in writing from the publisher. Printed in the United States of America.

The Haworth Press, Inc., 28 East 22 Street, New York, NY 10010

Library of Congress Cataloging in Publication Data
Main entry under title:

Reference services and technical services, interactions in library practice.

"Has also been published as the Reference Librarian, number 9, fall/winter 1983"—T.p. verso.
Includes bibliographical references.
1. References services (Libraries)—Addresses, essays, lectures. 2. Processing (Libraries)—Addresses, essays, lectures. 3. Libraries and readers—Addresses, essays, lectures. 4. Cataloging—Addresses, essays, lectures.
I. Stevenson, Gordon, 1924- . II. Stevenson, Sally. III. Reference librarian.
Z711.R4493   1984   025.5'2   83-22790
ISBN 0-86656-174-9

Reference Services and Technical Services: Interactions in Library Practice

The Reference Librarian
Number 9

CONTENTS

INTRODUCTION

The Nature of the Problem, If It Is a Problem   3
Gordon Stevenson

HISTORICAL BACKGROUND

View from the Top: The Library Administrator's Changing Perspective on Standardization Schemes and Cataloging Practices in American Libraries, 1891–1901   11
Wayne A. Wiegand

AN OVERVIEW

Current Issues in Technical Services   31
Gordon Stevenson

    Administrative Arrangements   33
    National Standards   35
    Complexity   36
    The Online Catalog   37
    Library of Congress Subject Headings   38
    Classification   38
    Conclusion   40

ORGANIZATIONAL ARRANGEMENTS

The Changing Roles and Relationships of Staff in Technical Services and Reference/Readers' Services in the Era of Online Public Access Catalogs   45
   Pauline A. Cochrane

The Ecumenical Library   55
   Michael Gorman

Noblesse Oblige: Collection Development as a Public Service Responsibility   65
   Larry Earl Bone

DOCUMENT DESCRIPTION

The Impact of AACR2 on the Harvard Library Union Catalog: A Case Study   77
   Carol F. Ishimoto

   The Union Catalog   77
   The DUC Standards   80
   The Impact of AACR2   82

Inter-Library Loan as an Unobtrusive Measure of Bibliographic Efficiency   89
   Sally Stevenson
   Gwen Deiber

Reference Services, Serials Cataloging, and the Patron   99
   Deborah J. Karpuk

   Organization   99
   Patron Confusion   100
   Control   101
   Public Service   102
   Reference Service   102
   Problem Solving   104
   Conclusion   105

SUBJECT ORGANIZATION AND ACCESS

The Flaw of Subject Access in the Library Catalog: An Opinion   109
    Norman D. Stevens

User Categories and User Convenience in Subject Cataloging   113
    Francis Miksa

Introduction	113
Cutter and User Convenience	114
User Categories: Shifting Ideas at the Turn of the Century	117
Library Differentiation by Size	119
Library Differentiation by Type	123
The Failure of User Categories Based on Types of Libraries	125
Observations	129

Where Have All the Moonies Gone?   133
    Sanford Berman

Descriptive Cataloging	136
Subject Cataloging	139

Classification Schemes as Cognitive Maps   145
    Richard A. Gray

The DDC and Its Users: Current Policies   155
    John A. Humphry
    Judith Kramer-Greene

Introduction	155
Change	157
Who Makes Major Policy Changes?	157
The Editorial Process	158
Responses to Users' Needs	160
Conclusion	161

READERS' FORUM

Personality, Knowledge, and the Reference Librarian   167
    Charles D. Patterson

FORTHCOMING IN THE REFERENCE LIBRARIAN   173

INTRODUCTION

The Nature of the Problem, If It Is a Problem

Gordon Stevenson

In any library with a staff large enough to permit the allocation of professional work according to special tasks, technical services librarians and reference librarians are partners in the common enterprise of providing services to the library's clientele. One would assume that these librarians work together very closely, and constantly interact in matters relating to the organization of the library's collections and the construction of the catalogs, indexes, and classification systems that provide bibliographical access to these collections. This, however, is not always the case, and in some instances it is almost never the case. If anything, the two specialties have tended to become more isolated rather than more integrated during the past several decades.

I suspect that more than a few reference librarians have worked in libraries where a serious exchange of ideas among specialists is more likely to revolve around the planning of a staff picnic than it is to revolve around the finer points of subject analysis. It is not surprising that some librarians have become a bit cynical about the impact of specialization. But the problem, if it is a problem, may have nothing to do with specialization as such, but with the way specialists are used, the way they are organized, and the way they interact. Specializations based on the distinction between public services and technical services probably evolved for good and sufficient reason. Whether the system should be continued in its present form is debatable.

Each of the specialties has defined its own role and each lays claim to special knowledge and skills. Sometimes this special knowledge is not as special as specialists like to think it is, but some of it is special to the point of being arcane. This, after all, is what we have come to expect of specialists in all professions. And, as often as not, with increased professionalization, specialties are broken down into sub-specialties (e.g., music cataloging, serials cataloging, reference work with children, government documents librarianship). Each group of specialists tends to become a "closed system," with much within-group communication but little if any between-group communication. Each specialty (and many sub-specialties) has its own professional organization, its own literature, its own mystique, its values, and its own ideas about what should constitute a proper education for librarianship.

In some cases, groups of specialists are cohesive enough to be identified as "sub-cultures," and there are "invisible colleges" that serve as channels of communication between widely dispersed specialists. It would not be unusual to find that a cataloger has more in common with another cataloger in a different state, even in a different country, than with a colleague working the reference desk in the same building. This is not an unimportant point—reference librarians reading this Introduction constantly use catalogs that were profoundly influenced in their basic structure by an international meeting that took place in Paris in 1961. This is the meeting that produced the Paris Principles, the foundation of AACR2.

In the case of cataloging and classification, there is a technical vocabulary that must be mastered if one is to talk to the specialists. What, for example, is a "corporate emanation" (the opposite of a corporate merger, perhaps?), what is a "distributed relative" (an uncle living in Florida?), or—heaven help us—a "hierarchically expressive notation" and a "retroactive notation"? Is such a vocabulary really necessary, or is it a secret code designed to turn platitudes into esoteric knowledge that is deliberately made incomprehensible to those outside of the group?

Catalogers and classifiers, on the other hand, could conceivably mistake one of those rather incredible flow charts of the reference process for a map of the London transit system. They might also think the literature on the "reference interview" a rather inflated—even pretentious—consideration of the obvious. In short, they are not likely to recognize the complex nature of communicative acts between strangers in public places, nor appreciate the subtle and complex cultural and psychological factors that inhibit or encourage face-to-face communications in the focused interview (it is even possible that there are some reference librarians who do not admit to these subtleties and complexities). Because of the behavioral dimensions to reference work, the reference librarian has quite a different frame of reference from the cataloger, with close ties to social-psychological aspects of communication as a dynamic process. It would appear that the theoretical foundations for the two specialties lie in quite different areas (whether this is the best situation is, of course, quite another matter). It is something of an anomaly that there is also a strong behavioral dimension to all systems of bibliographic organization, but this dimension seems to have had a minimal impact on the construction and evaluation of our traditional systems.

Public service librarians and technical service librarians do indeed see the world from different perspectives. They also see different parts of the world. One can understand why each may tend to underestimate the structural complexities involved in the work of their colleagues in other service departments. They are looking in two different directions, one towards individual users of libraries (who exist in cultural environments, display endless variables, and create unpredictable situations), the other looking towards the broad field of bibliographic organization, which today consists of a number of national and international systems which seem to be governed by their own internal laws. The goals of the reference librarian create a centripetal force, pulling a variety of elements together so they focus on an individual transaction. The work of the cataloger is governed by factors that create a centrifugal force, directing one's attention away from the single interaction to the universal and the general.

Different personal characteristics are ascribed to practitioners of the two specialties. Reference librarians "like to work with people," whereas catalogers "like to work with books." At least this is what we are constantly told, but as far as we know this is one of the untested assumptions of the folklore of librarianship. Even if this cliché turned out to be true, it is hard to imagine what value the information would be to anyone. More important are questions of cognitive style in information seeking, but little research has been done in this area. Studies in cognitive style would probably give us some insight into why and how some librarians are successful reference librarians and others are successful catalogers.[1]

One is tempted to suggest that we have two major areas of specialization because we have two major types of librarians—those who "like books" and those who "like people." There may be a grain of truth in this, but the reasons are probably more profound.

Our current arrangements for the allocation of responsibilities for the various parts of a library's information system are the result of

(1) certain historical factors (some of which date back to before 1900), (2) the unquestioned need for specialization (which is one of the distinguishing features of the organization of life in the twentieth century), (3) the economic advantages of specialization (which is in some ways comparable to the role of the assembly line in manufacturing systems—and originated around the same time), (4) the enormous complexity that must be dealt with in the construction of universal systems for the bibliographic control of the world's graphic records, and (5) as noted above, the most divisive and in some ways the most dysfunctional factor: the inexorable rise of national and international standards for not only network development but also for the bibliographic and bibliothecal organization of local collections, large and small.

Problems with our current arrangements have frequently been noted, and attempts have been made and are being made to find more productive alternatives. But in most libraries, the advantages of specialization are still thought to outweigh its disadvantages, and this may very well be the case. One also suspects that librarians themselves are largely content with the system. To change it would mean the loss of a certain part of one's professional identity, and most certainly would require the acquisition of many new skills.

From a managerial point of view, the first really important question that must be answered is this: are reference librarians, other public service librarians, and bibliographers getting the tools and systems they need to make the best use of their collections and other collections to which they have access? And if not, why not? Thus, under present organizational arrangements, the burden seems to fall to technical services librarians to make whatever changes are necessary to contribute more productively to the achievement of the library's service goals. This, however, is more easily said than done. Through no fault of their own, catalogers and classifiers can not do much to change bibliographic systems at the local level given the restraints placed on them by the nature of the standards with which they must work.

If the current system of specialization is not the best possible system, then what are the alternatives? Several alternatives are suggested in this issue of *The Reference Librarian*. But widespread and radical change seems rather unlikely in the near future. The current system is firmly entrenched in the very structure of the profession. In the meantime, whatever tensions exist in reference services vis-à-vis technical services may be alleviated to some extent if the two groups of specialists involve themselves in each other's specialties. The papers which follow are a step in that direction.

A number of librarians with different points of view, different backgrounds, and different specialties (including several library administrators) comment on various aspects of the relationships—current and potential—between the two service areas.[2] We have included several case studies: the impact of AACR2 on the union catalog of a very large university; the impact of AACR2 (and other factors) on the inter-library loan services; and the relationship between serials cataloging and reference services. Many librarians believe that the Dewey Decimal Classification is a basic tool in the provision of reference services, so we have included two articles about this system. One cannot talk about subject access in libraries of the United States without examining the Library of Congress subject headings. The material we have included should be most useful to reference librarians in understanding what it is they are dealing with when they use this system. Most of these issues are best understood when considered against an historical background, or such in any case is the conviction of the Editors of this issue. We begin, then, with a discussion of certain events that took place almost eighty years ago, and which left a very long shadow. At the end, we have included a response to an article published in an earlier issue of *The Reference Librarian* that deals with certain qualifications and characteristics of the reference librarian.

NOTES

1. A nice model for research in the cognitive styles of librarians, particularly comparative studies of reference and technical service librarians, is found in Alfred G. Smith's *Cognitive Styles in Law Schools* (Austin: University of Texas Press, 1979). Such a study might, in fact, tell us more about ourselves than we want to know.

2. We were recently saddened by the death of Neal Edgar, a much valued colleague who had planned to contribute to this issue of *The Reference Librarian*.

HISTORICAL BACKGROUND

View from the Top: The Library Administrator's Changing Perspective on Standardization Schemes and Cataloging Practices in American Libraries, 1891-1901

Wayne A. Wiegand

In the preface to a work entitled *Subject Headings* (1946), author Julia Pettee reflects on the state of cataloging science in 1895, the same year she graduated from the Pratt Institute Library School. "To the rank and file of catalogers," she writes, "the idea that the dictionary catalog had any relation to a systematic classification of knowledge had not dawned. We revelled in the new A.L.A. *List of Subject Headings* then just published."[1] With the benefit of hindsight, Pettee's last sentence reveals more than she recognizes. First, it implicitly acknowledges a changing environment surrounding the nation's library community at the beginning of the Progressive era. Second, it provides a partial explanation for the movement away from an emphasis on the individual library uniqueness which characterized the nineteenth century library and towards an emphasis on the general library standardization which characterized its twentieth century successor.

Wayne A. Wiegand is Associate Professor, College of Library and Information Science, University of Kentucky.

In 1895 Julia Pettee represented a new generation of librarians. She was a young female beginning professional cataloger trained in one of the nation's three library schools to institutionalize systematic classification. She was also conditioned to accept with little question or criticism a list of subject headings developed by a group of culturally homogeneous men acting within a professional association which had already presumed to speak for the nation's library community for nearly two decades.

How different were her words from the comments of William Isaac Fletcher, who wrote in *Public Libraries in the United States* (1894): "Every library has its own character and its own peculiar needs to meet; and the classification proper to any library is such an arrangement of its books as is best suited to its own circumstances."[2] Fletcher was in the autumn of his career as director of the Amherst College Library. He typified a passing generation of male professionals known as "scholar-librarians" who had no formal library training—in fact, who did not see the need of it—but who knew their collections first hand because they had cataloged most of the materials their libraries had acquired. Men like these even considered the advent of common cataloging principles suspect. Frederick Vinton, director of the Princeton University Library, boldly stated in *Library Journal* in 1877 that "cooperative cataloging... is unfavorable to good librarianship. For myself, I would on no account lose that familiarity with the subjects and even places of my books which results from having cataloged and located every one."[3]

Although the generation represented by Fletcher and Vinton dominated the politics and defined the direction of the American Library Association during its first fifteen years of existence, a variety of factors forced it to relinquish control to leaders of Pettee's generation between 1891 and 1901. During that decade library administrators increasingly looked to standardization as a solution to many of the cataloging and classification problems they faced. By examining the actions they took and the decisions they made, the library historian may be able to discover the origins of many of the difficulties separating contemporary technical and public service departments. This essay is an attempt to recount this watershed decade in our professional history.

The group of leaders which emerged from the organization of the American Library Association in 1876, and which controlled it by occupying positions on its executive board through 1893, was amazingly homogeneous. Ninety percent came from families which had been in the United States for more than three generations, and three-fourths could trace their origins to northwest Europe. Sixty-five percent were Protestant; the remainder were unaffiliated or their religious persuasion unknown. Three-fourths had no declared political affiliation; four-fifths were chief executives in the libraries employing them. All were males born in the Northeast; half were born to families in which the father occupied an important managerial position. Two of three came to librarianship from another profession. Three of four possessed at least undergraduate degrees, and 75 percent of those who did earned these degrees at Ivy League institutions. None, however, had any formal library science training.[4] The picture which surfaces from this collective profile depicts an accurate stereotype: the association was run by white Anglo-Saxon Protestant male library administrators.

Most of these administrators, however, came to their executive positions after a period of apprenticeship of some sort. During that period they were exposed to a variety of classification schemes governing the organization of nineteenth century American libraries, and to the different subject and descriptive cataloging principles which ruled the recording and detail of a collection's contents in the library's catalogs. Naturally, these apprentices applied what they learned to the collections they inherited when they became library administrators, but they also worked to correct shortcomings and modify the direction of the classification schemes and cataloging principles in order to address what they interpreted were the needs of their user publics. Such a service philosophy probably sparked Fletcher's call for an arrangement "best suited to [a library's] own circumstances."

The process of cataloging and classifying acquisitions automatically forced a knowledge of the collection's contents on the minds of the administrators themselves. Ainsworth Rand Spofford, Librarian of Congress from 1864 to 1897, built his reputation on his ability to retrieve the correct title from among the hundreds of thousands committed to his care. In fact, he resisted suggestions to delegate authority for cataloging and classification to others precisely because he feared that losing contact with LC's collections would make him a less effective librarian.[5] In an era in which a library's publics who paid the bills made a more direct contribution to decisions, as was the case in social, circulating, proprietary and in special libraries like LC in 1875, such reluctance to relinquish control, or, to use Vinton's line of logic, such a commitment to preserve "familiarity," is understandable.

Nonetheless, a movement for the standardization of subject headings and descriptive cataloging rules and a recognition of the value of uniform classification schemes persisted against this inertia. As early as 1852 Charles Coffin Jewett, director of the Smithsonian Library, argued for standardization of cataloging rules in his *On the Construction of Catalogues of Libraries*.[6] In 1876 Charles Ammi Cutter issued his *Rules for a Printed Dictionary Catalogue*, a move reinforced by the publication in five volumes of the *Catalogue of the Library of the Boston Athenaeum*,[7] the institution over which he presided. And in 1876, the newly formed American Library Association established a "cooperative committee" to discuss cooperative cataloging codes. But progress was slow, in part because leaders like Chicago Public Library Director William Frederick Poole, an ALA Vice-President, resisted. At the 1877 ALA conference he bristled at the committee's report on proposed rules for cooperative cataloging. "I do not propose to be bound by anything that this Association may do in this matter," he said. "I would rather the ALA should not commit itself to any particular style." Poole's attitude had a chilling effect. Committees appointed to discuss the feasibility of cooperative ventures showed little energy. ALA Secretary Melvil Dewey, who championed cooperation and systematization, forewarned President Justin Winsor against high expectations for the 1879 conference. Most of the committees, Dewey noted sadly, "are not doing anything."[8]

If Dewey expected comfort and sympathy from Winsor, he got none. Winsor and Poole were cut from the same professional cloth. Before coming to Harvard as library director in 1877, Winsor served in the same capacity at the Boston Public Library for nine years. There he carved a reputation as the nation's most influential librarian, in part because he led the prototype institution in the vanguard of a public library movement, in part because of the steady stream of historical scholarship which flowed from his pen. And because the volume of his publications increased dramatically after going to Harvard, he became the model for the "scholar-librarian" against which others measured their performance as ideal academic librarians.[9]

While Winsor could not support Dewey's suggestions for uniform cataloging rules and common classification schemes, he could support the dictionary catalog Cutter advocated so forcefully and convincingly. Cutter was also supported by Poole, Spofford and other nationally prominent librarians. In fact, at dedication ceremonies for the new library at the University of Michigan on December 12, 1883, Winsor articulated the contemporary professional consensus on the power and value of the dictionary catalog. "There is no factor in the efficiency of the library equal to the catalog," he said.

> It used to be the librarian. Van den Weyer in 1849, in his remarks before the Royal Commission at the British Museum, when some librarians were raising all sorts of objections against the preparation of even author's catalogues, met them squarely when he told them that the librarians who undervalued catalogues were aiming to make themselves personally indispensable. It was a telling blow at the traditional librarian and it was the truth. The race is not yet dead, and I could name one or two in this country.[10]

Winsor's words reflected a widespread confidence in the ability of the dictionary catalog to meet the information needs of the late nineteenth century library patron efficiently.

Although ALA leaders presumed to speak for a national library community about the value of a dictionary catalog, they could not divorce that community from changes and pressures in the larger social context from which it emerged. "Efficiency" became a watchword for Progressive reformers bent upon solving the social ills besetting late nineteenth century America. Many observers traced the origins of these problems to the effects of urbanization, immigration, and industrialization, and to the changing societal values fostered by each. Fearing the potential for disorder which could arise from this perplexing mix of forces, people manifesting the same socioeconomic profile as the ALA executives described earlier in this essay launched a series of social crusades to influence and, if possible, to control the social behavior of the poor, immigrant, urban, frequently unemployed worker and his family. Some crusades were more vigorous than others, as historians of movements to counter prostitution, pornography, the consumption of alcohol, and other "social vices" have pointed out. Some of these reformers carved out specialized areas of endeavor which they called "professions," and by attacking problems in a quiet, systematic, efficient manner using methods and skills acquired in university training, they claimed increased social status for themselves. Nurses, social workers, public health officials and city planners represented only a few of the scores of professions surfacing at this time.[11]

Librarians represented another infant profession claiming a unique place among the new groups of reformers. The library community shared a belief in the social benefits of reading good books, and its members dedicated their professional efforts to selecting these works. They assumed that citizens reading good books would make wise decisions about their employers, the politicians they elected, the places they chose to live, and the way they conducted their lives and raised their families. In 1876 the innovative library administrator of the first generation of "professionals" was expected to link the "proper" books bearing a socially beneficent message with the patron who had a particular information need. Because patrons commonly lacked access to catalogs and collections, and were generally ignorant of the classification schemes (and sometimes subject heading systems) unique to each library, the librarian, to paraphrase Winsor, had made himself "indispensable." But as the years passed in the last quarter of the nineteenth century, this situation changed. Library administrators became subject to increased demands upon their time, and slowly they began to rely more and more on the dictionary catalog as the primary patron guide to the information available in their libraries.

Although their belief in the efficacy of the dictionary catalog may have been naive, their conviction that libraries, and especially public libraries, had a socially useful but essentially passive role to play in reforming late nineteenth century America must have been convincing. In fact, it did spark a public library "movement" which the benefactions of philanthropist Andrew Carnegie greatly accelerated. Carnegie found the inherent passive nature of the public library especially attractive. People were not *forced* to come to the public library, he noted, but if they wanted to advance themselves, if they were self-starters (like himself), the public library could provide the foundation for building success in an age convinced of the irreversibility of social Darwinian "laws."

Driven by such convictions, the construction of libraries proliferated. In 1876 the U.S. Bureau of Education located and reported data on 3,600 libraries of all types with three hundred volumes or more. By 1900, less than a quarter century later, the bureau reported 5,400 libraries (*excluding* academic) with one thousand volumes or more. Carnegie alone donated more than $41,000,000 for the construction of 1,679 public library buildings before he died in 1919.[12] Naturally, the acceleration of public library construction also created some needs. All these libraries required staffing; and their buildings had to have collections suitably arranged for easy retrieval. But as librarians approached the turn of the century, the apprentice system proved unable to supply the number necessary to staff the new and growing libraries. Nor could the nation's library leaders come to agree upon a common classification scheme which all libraries might adopt.

Concomitant with this development in the arena of public librarianship came changes in higher education which altered demands made upon college and university libraries. A generation of American scholars trained in European graduate schools returned home to press institutions which hired them to encourage more independent student research. As a result, curricular requirements became more liberalized, and students were permitted to take more and more elective courses. Added to this pressure from inside the institution was another change taking place on the outside—the rise of professions. Many of the new professions looked for a university degree to sanction the formal training they required for admission to vocational circles they themselves restricted. Both of these developments pressed the libraries servicing the academic institutions at which they took place to expand their hours and their collections. The pressure was so great that Raymond Cazallis Davis, who directed the University of Michigan Library from 1877 to 1905, noted at the end of his career: "If I were asked to characterize in a few words my work as librarian, my answer would be ready; *A struggle for books.*"[13] Naturally, increased hours and rapidly expanding collections necessitated expanding staff.

How did the public and academic library communities respond to the pressures which these demands brought? At first tentatively, because the generation of professionals represented by Winsor, Poole, Vinton and Spofford continued to argue that a simple dictionary catalog listing the contents of the libraries over which they presided was adequate to their patrons' needs. Part of their rationale may have been wishful thinking—a quick mental response to a conscience which asked why they needed to spend more and more time on acquisitions work and administrative duties, and less and less time on direct service to patrons. They also seemed blissfully unaware that the apprenticeship system which had filled staff needs adequately before 1876 would be unable to process the numbers necessary to staff libraries with trained personnel in the last decade of the nineteenth century. As the twentieth century drew near, it became apparent to leaders of the next generation that new, more efficient, approaches were needed.

In the vanguard among those recommending change was Melvil Dewey, author of *A Classification and Subject Index for Cataloging and Arranging the Books and Pamphlets of a Library* (1876), director of the Columbia College Library from 1883 to 1888, director of the New York State Library and Library School from 1889 to 1905, and secretary of the American Library Association from 1876 to 1891. He served as ALA President in 1892-1893, and organized the very successful ALA conference and exhibit at the 1893 Chicago World's Fair. Dewey was the library profession's foremost apostle of efficiency, the watchword behind which many Progressive era social reformers paraded in efforts to justify their existence.[14] From the beginning, he prodded ALA to take the lead in devising cooperative cataloging rules, in agreeing upon a common classification scheme (of course, he assumed ALA would officially sanction his own Decimal Classification), and in identifying common library forms and appliances. Such efforts would reduce duplication of effort and minimize costs, he argued, and everyone would benefit. While Winsor and Poole controlled ALA, however, Dewey could make little progress.

Although ALA proved stubborn to his cries for cooperation, Dewey experienced marked success in structuring library education. In 1883 he announced that Columbia College was considering a library school. He solicited ALA's official blessing, but was spurned. ALA would only compliment Columbia on its willingness to experiment. Undaunted, Dewey pushed ahead with his own plans. On January 5, 1887, he formally opened the "School of Library Economy" to twenty students, only three of them men. The curriculum he designed emphasized technical training, with an emphasis on universally acceptable classification schemes and common cataloging rules which would make libraries more efficient and standardize their methods. Dewey admitted the curriculum was also intended to duplicate the end results of the apprenticeship system, but he argued the library school could accomplish the task more effectively and in less time.[15]

When Dewey pulled the library school out of Columbia and relocated it in Albany after he moved there in 1889, students did not suffer. Dewey never had any trouble placing his graduates in library positions across the country. A surprising proportion of the females took cataloging positions, and many of these traveled from library to library on four to six month appointments classifying (and in many cases reclassifying) collections in DDC. Several of Dewey's prize students set up other library schools in New York, Philadelphia and Chicago, and each mimed the curriculum Dewey inaugurated in Albany. Each school also showed enrollments consisting of mostly women, a large number of whom graduated into cataloging positions where they dutifully classified the collections under their care in DDC. Pettee later recalled:

> When the Dewey classification came into the field, the alphabetical-classed catalog and all of the various older combinations of author lists combined with classed or alphabetical subject indexes on cards disappeared. Libraries for the most part did a total job of reorganization, recataloging as well as reclassing.

Dewey had taught his "girls" well. By 1900, just under one third of the 377 graduates of these schools were still employed as catalogers. That the vast majority of them were women represents a significant factor in explaining the movement towards standardized classification schemes, subject headings, and common cataloging practices.[16]

Eventually, as Dewey's graduates (and the graduates of his graduates) began to populate the library world, they also joined the American Library Association, thereby giving Dewey the loyal constituency he lacked during ALA's first fifteen years. New leaders more sympathetic to the benefits of efficiency and standardization evident in cooperative cataloging, uniform lists of subject headings, and common classification schemes slowly rose into the ALA hierarchy. In terms of their socioeconomic profile, they did not differ substantially from the generation of library leaders typified by Winsor and Poole, but they had come to professional maturity in a growth environment which forced their attention to acquisition and administrative matters. The schemes Dewey pushed were more attractive to them.

Evidence of a shift already began to surface in the mid-1880s. Whereas a "committee on publishers' title-slips" could not get standardized entries in the "title-slip registry" which *Publisher's Week-*

ly issued in 1880 accepted by enough librarians to carry the project, by 1883 the ALA's "Condensed Rules for an Author and Title Catalog" issued by the cooperative committee enjoyed moderate success. Then, when ALA organized a publishing section in 1886, the association created a built-in mechanism to influence standardization of library methods and increase efficiency. Naturally, Dewey took a leading role in the development of the publishing section. He readily understood its potential for the small libraries recently established throughout the country which were desperately in need of guidance. Cooperative cataloging and common classification schemes promised a partial answer to the needs of their staff members who did not have the benefit of formal library school training.

As might be expected in an era of collection growth, first off the presses for the publishing section were acquisition guides like John F. Sargent's *Reading for the Young* (1890), an annotated booklist for young people. But soon members began to talk about other ventures. One scheme called for an *ALA Index* to record and control the many "good" essays lost to users whose only access to anthologies was now a dictionary catalog unit record too abbreviated to list them all. Despite big plans, however, the publishing section met mixed success. Bibliographies and indexes generally broke even; plans to launch cooperative cataloging efforts repeatedly met failure. William Coolidge Lane, secretary-treasurer of the publishing section and the assistant director of the Harvard College Library who would soon succeed Cutter at the Boston Athenaeum, found out why. In 1893 he reported the results of a survey of fifty-eight libraries which showed only five adhering to a single code absolutely. Most libraries used the ALA's "Condensed Rules for an Author and Title Catalog" merely as a general guide. Later that same year the Library Bureau, a library supplies company in which Dewey and his wife held majority stock, advertised "Printed Catalog Cards for Current Books/A Guaranteed Fact, Not a Mere Experiment." But because the bureau depended upon book publishers to send free advance copies of books, turnaround time on sending the cards to the forty-nine libraries which subscribed to the service was often excessive; many subscribers complained.[17]

A glance at the officers elected to the executive board of the publishing section in 1893 is revealing. Dewey, director of the New York State Library and the New York State Library School, became president; Lane, director of the Boston Athenaeum, remained secretary-treasurer. Other members of the board included Fletcher, who was editing the *ALA Index*, R. R. Bowker, editor of the *Library Journal*, and George Iles, an independently wealthy journalist and a library trustee who had recently agreed to donate to the production costs of an American history bibliography that Buffalo (NY) Public Library Director Josephus Nelson Larned would publish under a publishing section imprint. The section elected no catalogers, and no women. Officers were mostly executives who represented a constituency interested in universally acceptable classification schemes because new demands upon their time had diverted their professional attention to acquisitions and administration.

A glance at the leadership of the association itself between 1892 and 1896 is also revealing. Although ALA was still being run by white Protestant Anglo-Saxon male library administrators who possessed the same socioeconomic profile as their predecessors, by now the nature of administrative work had changed. Winsor, Poole and Cutter served as ALA presidents between 1876 and 1889, but from 1891 to 1896 the presidential office was occupied by Dewey, Larned, Henry M. Utley of the Detroit Public Library, John Cotton Dana of the Denver Public Library, and William Howard Brett of the Cleveland Public Library. All were chief executives, all public librarians, all structuring library systems in growing urban communities which made heavy demands on the collections under their care. Cooperative cataloging and universal classification schemes made sense to them, and the women they hired from library schools were eager to practice the techniques in cataloging they learned there. It all smacked of the efficiency, systematization and scientific management characteristic of a profession building a constituency in the Progressive era.

Comments and criticisms of the "old guard" also suggested the torch was passing from one generation to the next. Winsor admitted he spent most of his time on historical scholarship, very little on librarianship, and was "not now enough in the swim of such things" to make a difference in ALA. Poole was being openly criticized by his own board of trustees at the Newberry Library for spending insufficient time on administration. His subordinates often complained he gave them no direction and did not properly coordinate routine library work. And consensus developed in the nation's capital that LC's collections had simply outgrown Spofford's ability to deal with them in the manner of the mid-nineteenth century library administrator. These observations surfaced at hearings on the Library of Congress held by a joint congressional committee in

1896, just before the library moved into its new quarters. Among those who testified were Dewey, Brett and Herbert Putnam, Director of the Boston Public Library. Within months Spofford agreed to step down to make room for a new Librarian of Congress.[18]

Little wonder, then, at Julia Pettee's delight at the new *A.L.A. List of Subject Headings* (1895), which had benefitted directly from Cutter's pioneering efforts at the Boston Athenaeum and which the ALA Publishing Section quickly turned into a profit-making venture—its first real success. The times were apparently ripe. A year later the section took over the Library Bureau's printed catalog card operation and turned a profit, although not on a scale originally hoped for. Subscriptions hovered around sixty, and many complained the publishing section produced too few cards for large libraries, too many for small libraries. Still, the section could not afford to allow libraries "individualistic selection" because the practice would prove too costly. Put simply, libraries were told "all or none." Most chose none, and the service limped along, awaiting a solution. The answer seemed obvious—centralized cataloging. To be a success, centralized cataloging had to take place at a large library with a high acquisitions rate, and other libraries had to be able to order cataloging data for individual books from the large library. When Herbert Putnam succeeded John R. Young as Librarian of Congress in 1899, he began to look into the possibility that the Library of Congress might assume that role. He had ambitions for LC which were more in tune with the needs of a new generation of library administrators in place at the turn of the century. He shared their concerns, goals, and visions of the future, but unlike them, he commanded a library and a budget with the direct power to do something which would benefit all libraries.

Coterminous with this development the ALA Publishing Section appointed an "advisory committee on cataloging rules" in December, 1900, and charged the group to reconcile differences between leading catalog codes. Catalogers who were invited to contribute ideas, criticisms, and suggestions naturally worked through existing forums, which in this case happened to be an ALA round table organized in their behalf. In 1901 the group petitioned the executive board to become a formal section of the association. J. C. M. Hanson, head of the cataloging division of the Library of Congress, was elected chair; Mary E. Hawley, cataloger at the John Crerar Library in Chicago, became secretary. The move to organize had advantages and disadvantages, both for the present and the future.

"This separate section provided a good forum for those most consistently interested in cataloging," one recent library historian accurately notes, "but also led to the separation and isolation of catalogers from administrators. Before 1900, cataloging was a concern of all ALA members, since the issues were discussed in general meetings."[19] While her observations about the consequences of the separation are accurate, she nonetheless fails to emphasize two important elements in this development. First, it openly acknowledged that changing demands on librarians had now forced them to departmentalize professional assignments in order to maximize efficiency and minimize duplication of effort. Second, it served to segregate professionals on the basis of sex. The vast majority of administrators of large libraries were men; the vast majority of catalogers in all libraries were women. The distinction was important, though not often conceded publicly.

In July, 1901, Putnam announced at an ALA meeting that the Library of Congress would sell copies of its printed cards at cost plus ten percent through the ALA Publishing Section, and do it for any or all of the titles LC cataloged into its collections. Since LC automatically received one copy of each work copyrighted in the United States, the proposal promised to serve most cataloging needs of every library in the country. The response was overwhelming, and the eagerness of librarians to accept the LC cataloging practices that had evolved from the ALA "advisory committee on cataloging rules,"[20] and their willingness to accept the subject headings LC used which had built upon the 1895 ALA list, permanently altered the state of cataloging science. On only one important issue did the nation's leading library administrators fail to reach consensus. The cards did not include standardized call numbers. The new classification scheme developed by the Library of Congress had not yet stood the test of time, and Putnam, upon the advice of his staff, refused to use DDC because LC considered it too inflexible for a large collection. Besides, by 1901 library school graduates who had honed their cataloging skills on DDC already occupied scores of cataloging positions across the country; their familiarity with the Dewey scheme insured a resistance to change, no matter how much pressure LC brought to bear upon them.

Within a short span of ten years, then, a series of developments took place which stamped their mark indelibly on American library development and chiseled a form of organization into existence which has resisted change for most of the twentieth century. White

Anglo-Saxon male large library administrators from families long established on the North American continent came to professional maturity during a time when society seemed to be demanding more libraries and larger collections, but not much larger staffs. To cut costs they used their national professional association to forge some common cataloging principles and identify appropriate subject headings to superimpose on their dictionary catalogs. That most of them shared the same socioeconomic background—thus shared the same vocabulary carrying codes and symbols whose meanings were clear to most members of their group—may explain the relative ease with which the latter task was effected. Once accomplished, however, these administrators left the technical details inherent in cataloging and classification activity to others—mostly to the female catalogers who had graduated from curricula forged by Dewey's pioneer school. Once placed in cataloging departments, these women tended to stay there for the remainder of their professional careers. Very few catalogers made their way through cataloging departments to the upper echelons of library administration; those who did were mostly men who, like other white Anglo-Saxon male large library administrators, tended to think that women possessed second rate minds best suited to the technical "housekeeping" details required of cataloging work.[21] Complaints, criticisms, or suggestions for improvement of library services which emanated from cataloging departments were thus not awarded the same weight in the head librarian's office as those from reference departments. And why should they be, library administrators asked. All libraries benefitted from standardization and common systems. They reduced costs in large libraries, and now that the systems and standards were in place, the smaller libraries which could not afford staff members who either worked through the old apprenticeship system or through the new formal training programs at least had the systems themselves for guidance. Employees of smaller libraries could now purchase ALA Publishing Section products and educate themselves; after 1901 they could even order standardized printed catalog cards from the Library of Congress.

Within a ten-year period the library profession had developed and organized into bureaucracies in response to changing demands. The large library bureaucratic organization model, with its male administrator, its female cataloging force, and an emerging reference department that served as a training ground for future administrators, became the model for other libraries to emulate. Like all bureaucracies it had its strong and weak points at the time of its creation. And while it solved many of the major problems for which it was developed in 1900, it also created a residue of unanticipated problems resistant to change. That many of these problems remain with us to the present day will be obvious from a careful reading of other essays in this issue.

NOTES

1. Julia Pettee, *Subject Headings: The History and Theory of the Alphabetical Subject Approach to Books* (New York: H. W. Wilson Company, 1946), p. 3.
2. William Isaac Fletcher, *Public Libraries in America* (Boston: Roberts Brothers, 1894), p. 52.
3. Frederic Vinton, "Hints for Improved Library Economy, Drawn from Usages at Princeton," *Library Journal* 2 (October, 1877), 53.
4. These statistics are displayed and discussed in more depth in Wayne A. Wiegand, "American Library Association Executive Board Members, 1876-1917: A Collective Profile," *Libri* 31 (August, 1981), 22-35.
5. For a more detailed account of Spofford's career as Librarian of Congress, see John Y. Cole (ed.), *Ainsworth Rand Spofford: Bookman and Librarian* (Littleton, CO: Libraries Unlimited, 1975), especially pp. 32-41.
6. Charles C. Jewett, *On the Construction of Catalogues of Libraries, and Their Publication by Means of Separate, Stereotyped Titles* (Washington: Smithsonian Institution, 1852), p. 14.
7. Charles A. Cutter, *Rules for a Printed Dictionary Catalogue* (Washington: Government Printing Office, 1876); and Charles A. Cutter (comp.), *Catalogue of the Library of the Boston Athenaeum, 1807-1871* 5v. (Boston: Boston Athenaeum, 1874-1882).
8. *Proceedings of the American Library Association Conference, 1877* (bound into *Library Journal*, 2 [1877]), 29: Dewey to Winsor, June 14, 1879, Justin Winsor Letters, bound into 1881 volume of *Library Journal* and located in the Rosary College Library, River Forest, Illinois.
9. For a more detailed analysis of Winsor's career, see Wayne Cutler and Michael H. Harris (eds.), *Justin Winsor: Scholar-Librarian* (Littleton, CO: Libraries Unlimited, 1980).
10. Justin Winsor, "An Address," in University of Michigan Library, *Public Exercises on the Completion of the Library Building of the University of Michigan, December 12, 1883* (Ann Arbor: Published by the University, 1884), p. 38, and found quoted in Samuel Rothstein, *The Development of Reference Services through Academic Traditions, Public Library Practice and Special Librarianship* (Chicago: American Library Association, 1955), pp. 24-25.
11. A large body of historical literature addressing the question of middle class efforts to insure "social order" and maintain "social control" has appeared in the last fifteen years. The seminal work which introduced this paradigm is Robert W. Wiebe, *The Search for Order, 1877-1920* (New York: Hill and Wang, 1967), especially Chapter 5. See also Allen F. Davis, *Spearheads for Reform: The Social Settlements and the Progressive Movement, 1890-1914* (New York: Oxford University Press, 1967), Mary O. Furner, *Advocacy and Objectivity: A Crisis in the Professionalization of American Social Science, 1865-1906* (Lexington, KY: University of Kentucky Press, 1975), Sally Gregory Kohlstedt, *The Formation of the American Scientific Community: The American Association for the Advancement of Science, 1848-1860* (Urbana, IL: University of Illinois Press, 1976), Thomas L. Haskell, *The Emergence of Professional Social Science: The American Social Science Association and the Nineteenth Century Crisis of Authority* (Urbana, IL: University of Illinois Press, 1976),

Paul Boyer, *Urban Masses and Moral Order in America, 1820-1920* (Cambridge, MA: Harvard University Press, 1978), T. Jackson Lears, *No Place of Grace: Antimodernism and the Transformation of American Culture, 1880-1920* (New York: Pantheon Books, 1981), and Alan Trachtenberg, *The Incorporation of America: Culture and Society in the Gilded Age* (New York: Hill and Wang, 1982).

12. U.S. Bureau of Education, *Public Libraries in the United States of America. Special Report, Part 1* (Washington: Government Printing Office, 1876); "Public, Society, and School Libraries in the United States of 1,000 Volumes and Over in 1900," in U.S. Bureau of Education, *Report of the Commissioner of Education for the Year 1899-1900* v. 1 (Washington: Government Printing Office, 1901), pp. 946-1165. For a comprehensive account of Carnegie's public library benefactions, see George S. Bobinski, *Carnegie Libraries: Their History and Impact on American Public Library Development* (Chicago: American Library Association, 1969).

13. University of Michigan Library, *Annual Report of the Librarian, 1905-1906* (Ann Arbor, MI: University of Michigan, 1906), p. 55. For background information on changes in higher education and the rise of professions in the last quarter of the nineteenth century, see Burton J. Bledstein, *The Culture of Professionalism: The Middle Class and the Development of Higher Education in America* (New York: W. W. Norton & Co., 1976), and essays in sections two and three of Alexandra Oleson and John Voss (eds.), *The Organization of Knowledge in Modern America, 1860-1920* (Baltimore: The Johns Hopkins University Press, 1979), pp. 51-406.

14. Melvil Dewey, *A Classification and Subject Index for Cataloguing and Arranging the Books and Pamphlets of a Library* (Amherst, MA: 1876). The title of his second edition is more descriptive of the scheme which came to be associated with his name. See Melvil Dewey, *Decimal Classification and Relative Index for Arranging, Cataloging and Indexing Public and Private Libraries, and for Pamphlets, Clippings, Notes, Scrap Books, Index Rerums, etc.*, 2nd ed., rev. and greatly enl. (Boston: Library Bureau, 1885). Dewey still lacks a definitive biography. The most recent account of his life is Sarah K. Vann (ed.), *Melvil Dewey: His Enduring Presence in Librarianship* (Littleton, CO: Libraries Unlimited, Inc., 1978). See also Marion Casey, "Efficiency, Taylorism and Libraries in Progressive America," *Journal of Library History* 16 (Spring, 1981), 265-279, for a good discussion of the impact of "efficiency" on the library world. The standard text on the concept is still Samuel Haber, *Efficiency and Uplift: Scientific Management in the Progressive Era, 1890-1920* (Chicago: University of Chicago Press, 1964).

15. For an excellent discussion of this phenomenon which accurately fits the development of library education into the context of the development of the training of other professionals, see Carl M. White, *A Historical Introduction to Library Education: Problems and Progress to 1951* (Metuchen, NJ: The Scarecrow Press, Inc., 1976), especially Chapters 2 and 3.

16. Pettee, *Subject Headings*, 41. Statistics are cited in Sarah Vann, *Training for Librarianship Before 1923: Education for Librarianship Prior to the Publication of Williamson's Report on Training for Library Service* (Chicago: American Library Association, 1961), pp. 94-95. The number of women in library work rose from 3,122 in 1900 to 14,714 in 1920. See U.S. Department of Commerce, *Women in Gainful Occupations, 1870-1920* (Washington: Government Printing Office, 1923), pp. 42, 45.

17. William C. Lane, "Cataloging," in Melvil Dewey (ed.), *Papers Prepared For the World's Library Congress* (Washington: Government Printing Office, 1896), pp. 835-849; *Library Journal* 18 (December, 1893), 528-30.

18. Winsor to Poole, March 20, 1893, William Frederick Poole Papers, Newberry Library, Chicago; Franklin MacVeagh (a Newberry Library Trustee) to Poole, March 27, 1893, copy found in Justin Winsor Papers, Massachusetts Historical Society, Boston; and Edith E. Clarke (Poole's cataloger at Newberry) to Dewey, July 5, 1893, Melvil Dewey Papers, Special Collections, Columbia University Library, New York. See also U.S. Congress. Joint Committee on the Library. *Condition of the Library of Congress.* (Senate Report, 1573). 54th Cong. 2d sess. (Washington: Government Printing Office, 1897).

19. Kathryn Luther Henderson, "Treated with a Degree of Uniformity and Common Sense: Descriptive Cataloging in the United States, 1876-1975," *Library Trends*, 25 (July, 1976), 230. For an excellent analysis of the historical development of the use of subject headings in American libraries, see Francis Miksa's recently published *The Subject in the Dictionary Catalog From Cutter to the Present* (Chicago: American Library Association, 1983).

20. The committee rules eventually led to the Anglo-American *Catalog Rules* published in 1908. See American Library Association and (British) Library Association (comps.), *Catalog Rules: Author and Title Entries* (Boston: ALA Publishing Board, 1908).

21. A fascinating body of secondary literature which examines the rise of female professionals during the Progressive era has been published during the past five years. My conclusions about the attitude towards women in the library profession were extrapolated from these works. See especially Barbara J. Harris, *Beyond Her Sphere: Women and the Professions in American History* (Westport, CT: Greenwood Press, 1978), Karen J. Blair, *The Clubwoman as Feminist: True Womanhood Redefined, 1868-1914* (New York: Holmes and Meier Publishers, Inc., 1980), Margaret Gibbons Wilson, *The American Woman in Transition: The Urban Influence, 1870-1920* (Westport, CT; Greenwood Press, 1979), Redding S. Sugg, Jr., *Motherteacher: The Feminization of American Education* (Charlottesville, VA: University Press of Virginia, 1978), Ellen Condliffe Lagemann, *A Generation of Women: Education in the Lives of Progressive Reformers* (Cambridge, MA: Harvard University Press, 1979), and Dee Garrison, *Apostles of Culture: The Public Librarian and American Society, 1876-1920* (New York: The Free Press, 1979), pp. 173-241.

AN OVERVIEW

Current Issues in Technical Services

Gordon Stevenson

If any single event may be said to have precipitated a deep concern with the impact of technical services on public services it was the publication of the second edition of the *Anglo-American Cataloguing Rules* (AACR2). Despite the furor raised by AACR2, there are other issues affecting or likely to affect the nature of interactions between technical services and public services, and they may be more important in terms of the improvement of public services than the rules for descriptive cataloging: (1) the growing dissatisfaction with Library of Congress subject headings (perhaps not so much a dissatisfaction with subject headings, which is nothing new, as the growing conviction that something really should be done, and can be done, to improve them), (2) the rise of the online catalog, with its promise of improved access systems and new search capabilities, (3) the well-known evidence of catalog search failures as reported in the classic catalog use studies, and (4) the indication, from more recent studies, that sophisticated users of libraries are more likely to make extensive subject searches in an online catalog (whereas the number of searches in the card catalog correlates negatively with the degree of subject specialization and subject expertise of the searcher). The impact of these issues, we believe, will lead to an emphasis on the analysis and improvement of systems of subject organization and access, two areas in which there has been remarkably little change and virtually no major innovations in over fifty

---

Gordon Stevenson is Associate Professor, School of Library and Information Science, State University of New York at Albany.

© 1984 by The Haworth Press, Inc. All rights reserved.

years (rather, there have been many innovations in classification and vocabulary control, but they have not been incorporated into our traditional systems for the most part). Nevertheless, it was AACR2 that was the catalyst that raised grave concerns about the bibliographic tools produced by technical service departments in conjunction with agencies of centralized cataloging. What have not yet been sorted out are criticisms based on the cost of implementing ACCR2 and those that relate quite specifically to the structure of given rules—the administrative concern with the economic impact of the new code seems to have tended to preclude a fair evaluation of the code as a code.

Last year, in commenting on the recent history of codes for descriptive cataloging, Susan K. Martin wrote that "the library profession has learned that cataloging rules, once the sole domain of the cataloger, often affect the entire institution and its scholarly community.[1] A lesson learned better late than never, one might add. Indeed, many library administrators were taken aback by the resounding impact of AACR2, and this happened after the fact, after the publication of the code and at the beginning of its implementation. Another library administrator, Patricia Battin, wrote: "Our institutions cannot afford another ACCR2."[2] It does appear that proprietary rights to decisions related to the structure of the rules of descriptive cataloging will no longer be (if they ever really were) entrusted exclusively to the catalogers. To whom will they be entrusted? That remains to be seen. But keep in mind that there have been historical precedents dealing with exactly the same issue (e.g., the massive negative reaction to the preliminary edition of the A.L.A. cataloging rules of 1941, which led to what was described as a "crisis in cataloging," but which blew over rather quickly and after which cataloging decisions again reverted to catalogers).

Now, all of this concern with AACR2 is not surprising, for the catalog of the local collection is too important in all public services to be taken lightly. On the other hand, what we are seeing may be only the beginning of a thorough critical review of other technical service operations. Descriptive cataloging rules, as we have pointed out, are not the only bibliographic standards that have been entrusted to catalogers. We could make a few minor changes in Martin's statement to indicate the larger impact of bibliographic operations on reference services: "the library profession has learned that *systems of descriptive and subject access*, once the sole domain of the cataloger, *always affect* the entire institution and its scholarly community." In the case of the public library, the community may not be scholarly, but is affected nonetheless.

The domain of the cataloger includes far more than the rules of descriptive cataloging, and all of this domain is going to come under very close scrutiny during the next few years. In addition to descriptive cataloging data, catalogers supply reference librarians with subject analyses of the library's book collection (using the Library of Congress subject headings), and they organize these books on shelves (using either the Library of Congress Classification or the Dewey Decimal Classification). They also organize systems of access to periodicals, government document collections, collections of material in microprint, sound recordings, and other sources of information used by reference librarians.

In constructing many of these systems, much of the intellectual work of technical services is not done at the local level, but at the national level, and sometimes at the international level. Thus, if a reference librarian is displeased with, say, the subject headings assigned to a given book, where does one lay the blame? Probably not with the local subject cataloger, because in most cases headings are supplied by catalogers at the Library of Congress. If one does not like the structure of a given heading, one's complaints are with the editors of the printed list of headings used by the Library of Congress. Therefore, when we talk about the inter-relationships between technical services and public services, we have to include national standards as part of the system.

Clearly, the use of national standards—as valuable and indispensable as they are for national systems and for network development—have some dysfunctional side effects. In some cases, our very idea about the possibilities and limitations of public service are defined by these standards. We have taken their limitations as a matter of course. This is not likely to be the case much longer. Here we will comment on a few of the major issues, questions, and other topics that are treated in more detail in the papers which follow.

ADMINISTRATIVE ARRANGEMENTS

Wayne Wiegand has shown that the system we use today to organize the skills and talents of librarians into a service-oriented system is based on patterns that were fairly well developed by around 1900.

Subsequently, the two major areas of specialization, public services and technical services, moved further apart, and new areas of specialization were added to the system. This was a rational development necessitated by the massive increase in the size of libraries, the development of new public services, the provision of services to new groups of users, and the increasing complexity of the world of knowledge. The movement in libraries was part and parcel of a larger nationwide movement towards bureaucratization, efficiency, and the standardization of virtually anything that could be standardized—all directed to the organization of the socioeconomic life in predictable and controlled systems. This is the milieu that produced the library as we largely know it today.

Have we reached the point where the broad range of technical services operations resulting from this movement and subsumed under the term "cataloging" have become so removed from the everyday functioning of libraries that they cannot respond to the needs of reference librarians? If this is the case—and some librarians think it is—then alternative systems of organization must be examined. And if changes are made, more than likely reference librarians will become much more directly involved in these "cataloging" activities.

There are two bits of evidence that say something about the present state of the relationships between technical services and reference services. This evidence is not presented here as definitive, but as something to think about.

1. A few years ago, one librarian wrote that the Library of Congress Classification is "the most workable tool at present available to carry forward the mundane but needful task of moving books and records from catalog departments to shelves and catalog."[3] This is one way to look at technical service operations. But what happens after those books and records are in the system? Is this not a concern of catalogers and classifiers? Apparently some technical service librarians think it is not.

2. The second bit of evidence is not related to the Library of Congress classification, but to the catalog: "Many librarians do not have a good understanding of the catalog, as evidenced by their own success in searching."[4] This information was a result of the A.L.A. catalog use study, and the general impression one gets on reading the study is that librarians had no more success with the library catalog than the typical library user. This is rather hard to believe, but if it is true, the situation is indeed quite grim.

NATIONAL STANDARDS

Of the rather large number of bibliographic standards that have an impact on the efficiency and quality of reference services, these seem to be the most important:

1. The Anglo-American Cataloguing Rules (AACR2)
2. Library of Congress subject headings (LCSH)
3. The Library of Congress Classification (LCC)
4. The Dewey Decimal Classification (DDC)

The rise of these standards has been one of the defining factors of contemporary librarianship in the United States. Few would argue that they have not been enormously important, for it is not likely that we could have any control over graphic records at the national level without them. But in accepting these standards we have seen the loss of some autonomy at the local level. The primary function of the "cataloger" is to interpret these standards and apply them locally. This is something quite different from a type of specialization in which the cataloger examines the needs of a given library and then constructs an appropriate system for that library.

Here is an example of the sort of issues that we should be concerned with: If all libraries use, say, the Library of Congress subject headings, this must be because we assume that local factors are not in any way unique, that such factors as these are not important in organizing systems of subject organization and access: the size of the collection, the nature of the collection in terms of subject specializations, and the needs of users. But everything we know about subject organization and access tells us that these things *are* important. When we reach the point where a small public library, or even a small college library with only a few hundred thousand volumes, uses the same system of subject headings as that used by a library, the Library of Congress, with many millions of volumes, it is time to examine the limits to which standardization is useful. In the case of, say, the Library of Congress classification, what are the consequences of using this system? Does anyone really know? I doubt it. Does the system encourage or inhibit subject access? Of what use is the system in reference work? It is not at all evident that such questions as these have been seriously dealt with. We seem to use Library of Congress subject headings and the Library of Congress Classification systems because they are there, because they are centrally applied, and relatively cheap to use. Not, one would think, the best rationalization for the use of any bibliographic system.

COMPLEXITY

To some reference librarians, the rules of AACR2 seem unduly complicated. Is this complexity necessary? Yes, we think it is. Consider the purpose of AACR2. This code is designed to provide a system for the descriptive cataloging of virtually everything ever published anywhere in the world (and even for unpublished materials), in any language, at any time, by any person or agency, in any form (e.g., book, periodical, etc.). To construct such a code for a single integrated system inevitably creates complications. Even though simplification is certainly possible at the local level in many cases, consider the function of the full code. The function of AACR2 is to provide a system that can serve as an international system for the construction of bibliographical records and their exchange by a system that is universally understood. The size of the potential data base it organizes is nothing less than everything published and much that is not published—many millions of titles.

If one were to use AACR2 exclusively as the foundation of a local system, then one could make many changes. One could, for example, simplify the rules for names of foreign and international corporate bodies; one could simplify the rules for the construction of uniform headings, particularly the more complicated rules necessary to organize large collections of printed music and sound recordings; and there are surely many other parts of the code that could be simplified. The complexity of the code is what one must accept if one wants to directly link one's local bibliographic system or one's bibliographic reference services to the national system.

There is also a cost to the reference librarian. It seems obvious that the most efficient users of the catalog must be the reference librarians (thus, they need to understand its basic principles, such as that of "corporate emanation"). As even catalogers must know, it is one thing to enter an item in an AACR2-based system, but it is quite another to find it once it is there. So, if the catalogers are the input experts, the reference librarians should be the experts in the actual use of the system. Reference librarians should know the AACR2 rules at least as well as the catalogers.

In the case of the complexities involved in modern principles of classification, most librarians in the United States have not had much reason to be concerned, for the state-of-the-art of classification as found in the Library of Congress Classification is that of the pre-modern era of classification. I doubt that learning the basic principles of faceted classification would be of much help in making better use of the Library of Congress Classification, but one might become interested in trying another system if one understood the potentials of faceted systems. If academic librarians in the United States are interested in the potentials of a modern classification system, and find the Dewey Decimal Classification unacceptable, they should examine the new edition of the Bliss Bibliographic Classification.

In the case of subject headings, do librarians understand what Cutter meant to do with the "syndetic structure" he wanted in his system? Can they evaluate the syndetic structure as it is now found in the Library of Congress system? Do librarians understand how and why in the post-Cutter era, parts of the system were changed to become a pseudo-alphabetico-classed catalog? The publication of ready-made lists of headings absolved subject catalogers from the need to understand the theoretical and structural foundations of the systems they apply.

A considerable amount of progress has been made during the past thirty years in the understanding of structural principles underlying efficient systematic vocabularies and classification systems. In fact, the principles are not particularly difficult to understand, and the more reference librarians become students of these disciplines, the more likelihood there will be of improving our traditional systems.

THE ONLINE CATALOG

It has been stated by a number of librarians that the online catalog will have more impact on the structure and quality of library services than any other innovation in more than a hundred years. Any assumption that online catalogs will use traditional subject access systems in their present form cannot be reconciled with the exploitation of the full potentials of automated subject access using controlled vocabularies and systems of classification. Thus, it is rather obvious that the online catalog is going to have an impact of the structure of subject headings. It is not yet so obvious, but soon will be, that there will be even more radical changes in our conception of the nature and uses of bibliographic classification.

LIBRARY OF CONGRESS SUBJECT HEADINGS

Of the various criticisms of the Library of Congress subject headings (LCSH) from practicing librarians, the most prevalent have been those relating to outdated headings, culturally-biased headings, and the lack of new headings for new subjects. Such problems are relatively easy to solve, and one is surprised at their persistence. More basic questions relate to the fundamental structural principles that underlie LCSH. Before much can be done to improve the system, it seems obvious that we must know what we are dealing with: what are these headings, how did we get them, how are they constructed, how could they be structured differently, how are they inter-related, in what ways are they internally inconsistent, why are they internally inconsistent?

It is quite remarkable that only in 1983 did we finally get a thorough analysis of the structural origins and history of LCSH, from the time of Cutter to the present. This detailed analytical study by Francis Miksa will—we predict—mark a turning point in the history of LCSH.[5] It is not likely that anything much can now be said about the structural aspects of LCSH without taking Miksa's work into account, and more than likely the bulk of what has been written about the system, if not outdated by Miksa's work, will be qualified and amplified by it. In this issue of *The Reference Librarian*, Miksa discusses one of the most important concepts that has shaped the structure of LCSH: the changing conception of the catalog user.

In the meantime, the Library of Congress has certainly not lost interest in LCSH. In recent years, the number of changes in the headings (changes for the better) has run into the thousands. Obviously, the Library of Congress has set about the job of making extensive improvements, including the examination of structural features and online potentials.

CLASSIFICATION

In this issue of *The Reference Librarian*, we have included two articles about the Dewey Decimal Classification (DDC): a critical review of certain aspects of the system, and a statement from the Forest Press explaining the methods by which the system is changed and updated.

Richard Gray is concerned with the use of classification as a "cognitive map," a guide to systematically thinking about one's collection, its contents and its structure. This use of classification is certainly one of the features of the DDC that has kept it alive and growing for over one hundred years, and the feature which will keep it alive for a long time to come. Reference librarians working in DDC-organized libraries clearly have a valuable tool at their disposal.

The Forest Press and the other individuals and agencies involved in the continuation of the DDC, during the course of the past several decades, have tried to develop an editorial system that makes every effort to be responsive to the needs of the users of the system. If they have not done this to the satisfaction of all concerned, keep in mind the vast number of libraries using the system (perhaps as many as 35,000 libraries throughout the world—and these are representative of many, many different types of libraries, both large and small).

The DDC is used in many countries as the basis for classified catalogs. The classified catalog has not been much of an issue in the United States since around 1900. Thus, we currently use classification only as a system for organizing books on shelves (that is, we use bibliothecal classification as opposed to bibliographic classification). Richard J. Hyman has urged that we need research in the uses of bibliothecal classification.[6] But, unfortunately, as cogent as Hyman's arguments are, we know of no major research in progress. Hyman's work deserves careful attention because, more than likely, the issue of the difference between bibliothecal and bibliographic classification is going to become extremely important with the rise of the online catalog.

Elaine Svenonius has recently shown how classification can be used for subject searching in online catalogs.[7] If the Forest Press can move ahead with research on the use of DDC in online subject searching, it is very possible that upcoming editions of the system will include some new features that will considerably improve online subject access. This may be the most significant change in the use of the DDC since its origins over a hundred years ago. Because of the inclusion of DDC class numbers (about 100,000 each year) for books added to the MARC data base, if search strategies can be worked out, anyone with access to the MARC data can use the system, regardless of what system they use to classify books in their own libraries. The prospects of such a system are considerably enhanced by the long-range possibility of subject access to material from some of the more than 130 countries world-wide that use the DDC. Svenonius suggested that the DDC can serve as a "switching language" at the international level—a topic of much concern to the International Federation of Library Associations as a means of improving subject access at the international level.

The Library of Congress Classification remains one of the great unsolved mysteries of twentieth-century librarianship in the United States. It is, in fact, even less known than LCSH was before Miksa's work. Practically nothing is known about how it is used, it has not been evaluated extensively as a shelving system, its theoretical foundations are obscure. Does it serve as a "cognitive map"? An interesting question, and perhaps someday someone will try to answer it. Advocates of the Library of Congress Classification consistently claim that "it works" and that it works very well. But *how* it works, *why* it works, and exactly what happens when it does work have not been much discussed in the library literature. The system seems to have remained completely impervious to any significant structural changes since the day it was first published. It seems hardly at all related to the mainstream of twentieth-century classification theory. How will it work in an online catalog? Will it do more than provide fragments of the shelflist? We suspect that we will soon get research results answering some of these questions.

CONCLUSION

We have commented on what we think are, or soon will be, important issues in technical services. The perspective has been that of the user of systems produced by technical services. There surely are other important issues, some crucial to the improvement of public services and others crucial to the efficient internal organization of the work of technical services. What seems to be evident is that the basic issue underlying all others is the nature of the inter-relationship between reference librarians and technical service librarians. The two groups of librarians should not work in isolation from each other.

REFERENCES

1. Susan K. Martin: "The Saga of Cataloging Rules," *Library Issues* 2 (March 1982), p. 4.

2. Patricia Battin: "On preparing competent professionals: Some advice to the King advisory group," *American Libraries* (January 1983), p. 24.

3. Raimund E. Matthis: "Moderator's Comments," in Jean M. Perreault, ed., *Reclassification: Rationale and Problems* (Conference Proceedings from the School of Library and Information Services, University of Maryland, vol 1). College Park: School of Library and Information Services, University of Maryland, 1968. p. 27.

4. F. W. Lancaster: *The Measurement and Evaluation of Library Services*. Washington, D.C.: Information Resources Press, 1978, p. 72.

5. Francis Miksa: *The Subject in the Dictionary Catalog from Cutter to the Present*. Chicago: American Library Association, 1983.

6. Richard J. Hyman: *Shelf Classification Research: Past, Present—Future?* Occasional Papers, no. 146. Champaign: University of Illinois, Graduate School of Library Science, 1980. Also see Hyman's *Shelf Access in Libraries*. Chicago: American Library Association, 1982.

7. Elaine Svenonius: "Use of Classification in Online Retrieval," *Library Resources & Technical Services* (January-March 1983), pp. 76-80.

ORGANIZATIONAL ARRANGEMENTS

The Changing Roles and Relationships of Staff in Technical Services and Reference/Readers' Services in the Era of Online Public Access Catalogs

Pauline A. Cochrane

Even as this is being written a Preconference to the 1983 A.L.A. Annual Conference is being held in Los Angeles with the title "Online Catalogs, Online Reference: Converging Trends." The speakers at that conference will be talking about services which would not even have been mentioned in passing at the 1973 Preconference on "Library Automation: The State of the Art II" held in Las Vegas.[1] Interestingly enough the same person helped to organize both conferences, Brett Butler, President of Information Access Company. In 1973 the emphasis of the papers presented was on technical services, the building of the data base, the role of the vendor, local systems, and national networks. Even the paper by Lois Kershner on "User Services" presented at that conference focused primarily on circulation systems and alluded to new "data base information dissemination services" which a few libraries and information centers had started (pp. 38-55). Several presentations at that Las

---

Pauline A. Cochrane is Professor, School of Information Studies, Syracuse University.

© 1984 by The Haworth Press, Inc. All rights reserved.

Vegas conference included predictions, many of which were quite correct. One was especially prescient when she said:

> The overall organization structure of the library may be materially altered as a library proceeds into its third or fifth operational year of library automation. . . . Another change which is not properly accommodated in the present organizational charts is how automation and the reference service or bibliographic functions will be integrated. A loose arrangement via a committee will not provide the proper clout for effecting those needed changes in personnel and objectives in the organization which is implicit in one policy statement: "point of use is point of input." (pp. 110-111, Atherton)

Another statement in that paper is also worth quoting: "The fast-response, computerized union catalogs and their ancillary network apparatus will do more to change our goals and attitudes, believe it or not, about *library service* than it has or will change our cataloging procedures" (p. 112).

It is obvious that a lot has happened in libraries which has irrevocably altered the focus of professional tasks away from technical services and toward public or reference services. From the announcement of the 1983 Preconference we learn that the pioneering efforts of the 60s and 70s are in place and working and that now the emphasis has to be on providing computer-based reference services *directly to the public*. One of the library automation pioneers, Frederick Kilgour, feels that the last ten years (1973-1983) represent a real departure from the usual trend of librarians' languid acceptance of technology. In a private communication he itemized the library innovations of the past century and a half (first card catalog in the 1830s, structured subject headings in 1843, magazine indexing in 1848, narrow subject classification in 1873, full-time reference service in 1884 and then a hiatus until the early 1930s when microphotographic techniques were implemented, followed by user-operated photocopying in 1960 and COM catalogs in 1966). He then contrasted that with the use of computer power in libraries in the 1970s, so much so that it is bringing libraries to the brink of a precedent-shattering socio-technological change, as "information seekers happily abandon their dependence on the traditional catalog with its single—or at most dual—linear arrangement of entries in favor of catalogs designed to provide a multitude of miniature catalogs of multi-dimensional design and accessible by many bibliographic and non-bibliographic avenues hitherto unavailable, and as they increasingly seek access to catalogs linked to electronic files of information by using personal computers in home, school and office." He does warn, however, as has this author in numerous places, that although computer power has improved and enhanced library efficiency, it has not shattered the basic library concepts of subject classification of materials, bibliographic description and headings for subject access.[2]

Are we about to see a fundamental shift in library tasks in this area which will shake up the allocation of tasks between the reference and technical services departments of libraries? Other professional groups have observed such trends and several sociologists have made early predictions about the library profession, e.g., Robert Presthus[3] and Philip Ennis.[4] This paper will address some of the issues surrounding such a shift and will also try to observe why the shift will be resisted.

During the early years of library automation the traditional bifurcated organizational chart of libraries was reinforced with automation systems personnel being added or appended to the Technical Services side of the house. Oftentimes the new library managers came from these ranks and continued to favor such an organization. The era of online public access catalogs and online reference services (dependent on systems *outside* the library) is changing all that. The reference staff have to be heard from because they are closer to the public users and their reports of problems must be addressed or the entire system could prove to be worthless. This same group is also involved in instructional programs for the users, promotional literature and other publications, user studies, and subject specialized products and services.

These augmented functions for reference service personnel have been having an effect on staff organization in special libraries for many years and there are now growing signs of library reorganization in public and academic libraries as well. If the traditional bifurcation is maintained, there is still growing recognition for the fact that Technical Services are "support work functions" and reference and circulation are seen as "user services." A more realistic organizational chart along functional lines would look more like the charts drawn for the *Handbook for Information Systems and Services*,[5] shown in Figures 1 and 2.

The deployment of subject specialists throughout the library or-

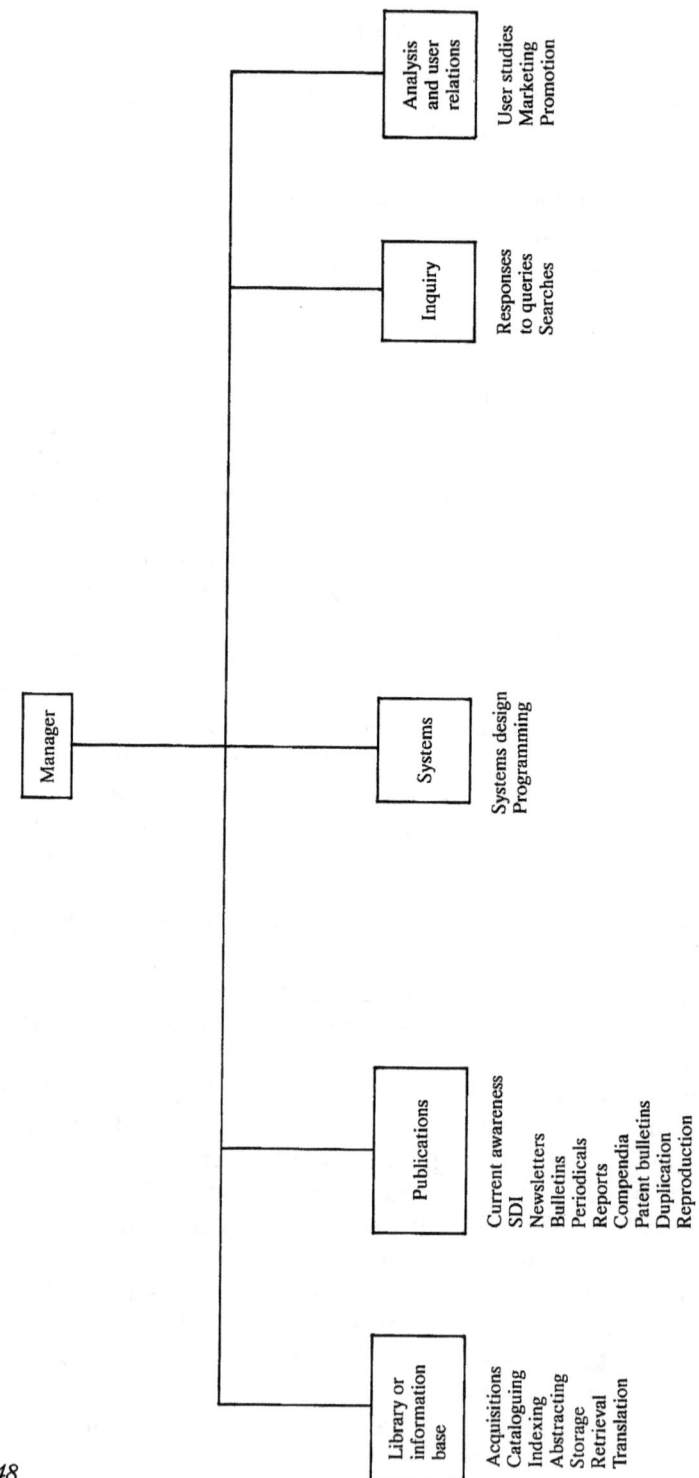

Organization of information services by functions

Figure 1

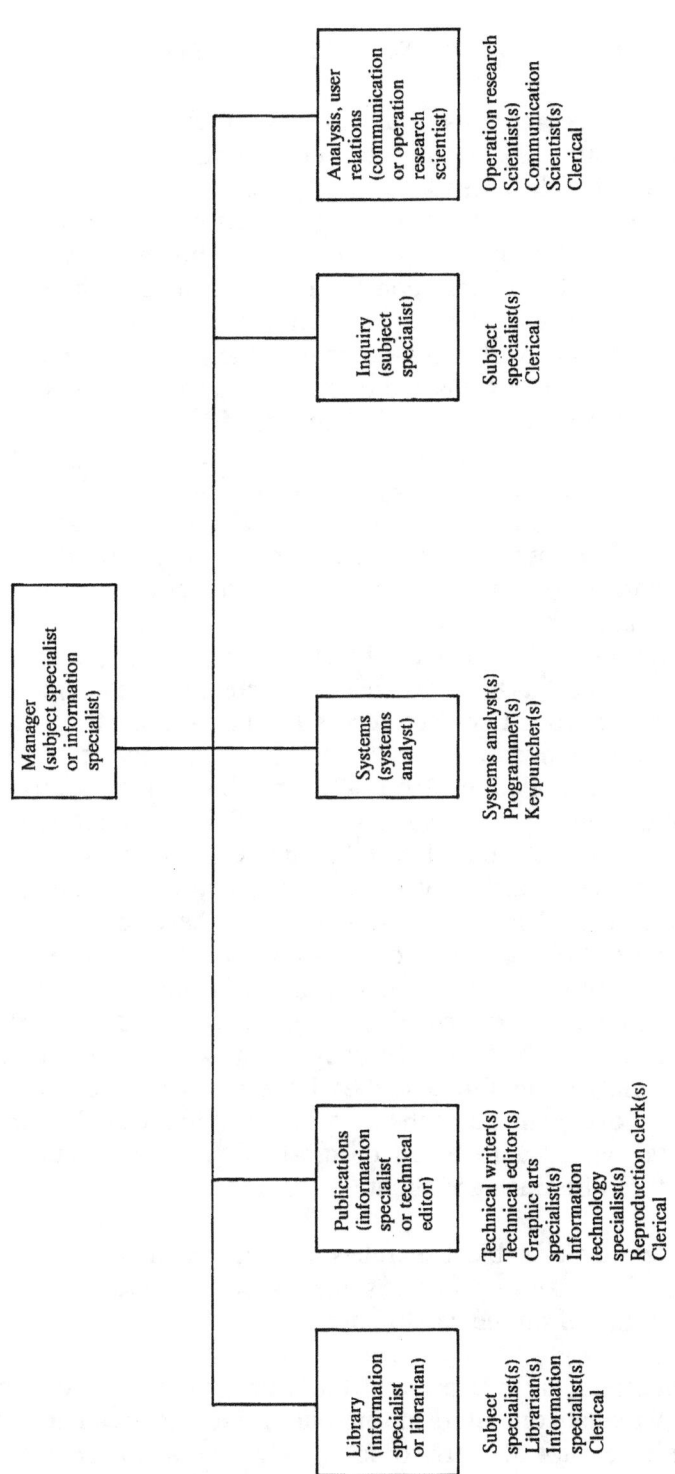

Manpower requirements of information services related to functions

Figure 2

ganization and the deemphasis of technical staff (systems analysts, catalogers, information specialists, etc.) are having profound effects on the make-up of task forces and other planning groups who are making decisions about online catalogs, network policies, and related budgetary and administrative decisions. This group has not yet had any perceptible effect upon the redesign of the cataloging record or the subject access tools surrounding the online catalog. This appears to be still within the domain of the technical services staff at the Library of Congress and elsewhere. Unfortunately these latter staff members do not feel in control either as they have adopted a "wait and see" attitude about online catalog design and development, hoping that a turnkey system will have all the bells and whistles needed to satisfy their user clientele. Developments at the Library of Congress have not been forthcoming even though Maurice Freedman (as early as the 1973 Preconference cited earlier), and others have noted the national dependence on the Library of Congress for name and subject authority data. As a result little innovative effort has been expended to accommodate the public user's need for improved subject access. In fact the contrary has been noted in a nationwide survey, in which online public access catalog users were polled in 1981-82. The Council on Library Resources Study, run by five organizations in 29 libraries across the United States, brought in some fairly damning evidence that "users of online public access catalogs want (and do not get) more sophisticated subject access."[6] Executive summaries of these researchers' findings are appendices to the report of a conference sponsored by The Council on Library Resources at the Aspen Institute, Wye Plantation in Queenstown, Maryland, December 14-16, 1982.[7] A forthcoming research paper by Karen Markey[8] discusses the three findings which stand out in these studies because they emerged in analyses from more than one of the methods used in the studies and were pervasive with regard to all or most of the online catalogs studied. The three findings are about:

1. preponderance of subject searches at online catalogs;
2. problems increasing output of subject searches; and
3. relearnability of online catalog use.

If the forecasters are correct and our library catalogs will be linked to the personal computers in four out of five American homes by 1990, we have a lot of work to do to overcome and correct the deficiencies in the first generation online public access catalogs which have just been surveyed. Some people are at work in such redesign efforts, but unfortunately, few of these efforts represent a coordinated national effort which would result in a universally adopted, professionally approved version of an online catalog. The period of experimentation, competition, and bandwagon effect will be the norm for several years to come.

Charles Hildreth of the OCLC Research Department, more than anyone else, has been following these developments with a critical eye and some constructive commentary.[9] Hildreth has developed a profile of first, second, and third generation online catalogs and an "OPAC Interface Adequacy Assessment Guide" which he presented at the 1983 American Library Association conference. A great many of the features he itemizes have to do with subject access, user-oriented displays of a subject vocabulary, tutorial features, and suggestive prompts, individualized displays, and the like.

To implement such changes will require technical expertise, to be sure, but it will also require some of the expertise which only the reference staff in a library can supply. Without inflating their knowledge and experience, it is this group to whom designers must turn for advice and counsel about user attitudes, skills, and expectations. Unfortunately, as a group, they do not yet have the research and development experience that technical services staff have in computer-based system design, communication research, and user requirements. They do not present a united front against the limitations of technology and automation, nor have they assumed the responsibility for the continuous effort to improve existing systems.

As the earlier organizational charts indicate, the personnel normally thought of as "reference librarians" can permeate other activities in a library (publications, user surveys, bibliographic instruction, management, etc.). They can even organize custom-built indexing and information services, but few have influenced the traditional world of subject cataloging and retrieval system design. That would appear to be the area where they are most needed as we move from the second to the third generation of online catalogs.

Why, one might ask, have reference librarians resisted the role they can play in improved online catalog design? Mary Lee Bundy presented a perceptive analysis of that question as early as 1968.[10] She mentioned the not ungrounded fear of job displacement and status or power loss. She also mentioned that libraries have very naturally attracted more than their share of people who could be described as ritualists, persons who overconform on the means of the organization, for whom indeed the means have become the ends, acquiescing to automation only to the extent that it does not seriously disturb the internal status quo. Any innovation in such an environment must be accomplished by those willing to make change in both established goals and procedures. In an essay co-authored with Paul Wasserman,[11] Bundy reviewed the intense peer pressure that discourages members of a profession from making public disclosures of undesirable practice, with intergroup rivalry, and a strong willingness to play an inexpert role. These authors were critical of the "phenomenon of the essential timidity of library practitioners, clearly reflected in the widespread, deep-seated and trained incapacity or high degree of reluctance to assume responsibility for solving information problems and providing unequivocal answers." The only bright light they saw on the horizon (in 1968) was an observation Bundy and Wasserman made about "individual librarians who have assumed significant information responsibilities for their constituencies. . . resulting in imaginative application of bibliographic expertise and subject competence."

The reluctance or ignorance of library managers during this early automation period resulted in an arrested effort to discuss or effect change in, or reassessment of, goals and services. Lacking leadership and a mode of communication, the bifurcated staffs in libraries did not effect change, review and reassess, or regroup and innovate.

Reference librarians as a group, or any subset of the group who expressed an interest in automation, have had their hands full in the past five to eight years just keeping up with the variation between and among the retrieval system vendors they have had to use to provide online reference retrieval. Very few have been directly involved in the local efforts to close the catalog in card or COM form and open the online catalog. Nevertheless, they have had to stand the brunt of user instruction in the use of the online catalog and they have had to redesign the informational brochures and help messages available online. Some of them have even made the effort to train the staff who also felt left out in the cold by the new form of the catalog. Given all these new chores and the added burdens, it is no wonder that they have not had time as a group to also attack the pending problems of improved subject access online. Carol Mandel and Judith Herschman[11] have sounded the alarm, but an across-the-board concerted effort has still not surfaced. Some have suggested enhancements of the cataloging record, others have suggested better related term displays than those provided by LCSH, and still others have opted for automatic indexing, weighting and relevance feedback techniques to be added to the software which makes up the online catalog. Where this scurrying will all lead is still not certain, but it is obvious that technical services staff can no longer consider themselves the only "data base managers" on the library staff. The *collective* efforts of reference librarians experienced in assisting and instructing the public users in the use of the online catalog and the catalogers and systems personnel responsible for the data base and access to it will be the only kind of team that can create an effective tool. Given the raw materials they have to work with (the MARC record, LCSH, and existing computer software upgraded from an online circulation system), they have a very tall order to fill.

To recapitulate, library staff members have tended to look at their professional tasks as bifurcated, with the builders of the catalog and the inventory keepers on one side and the middlemen or customer representatives on the other side. The online catalog is changing all that because this tool needs to be fashioned by a collaborative effort. Data elements in the catalog record and auxiliary files like a subject authority file will need to be refashioned to make information more accessible and user effort minimal. Certainty of success when the catalog is used at remote locations will be paramount or adverse user reaction will topple the system.

Library managers are beginning to realize that library goals are shifting away from collection development for its own sake to a more moderated view about the importance of collection management and development, given that user satisfaction is quantifiable and measurable, even at budget time.

Reference staff are beginning to take on the responsibility for online catalog design and improvements in subject access tools. If not as a group, then perhaps as groups of subject specialists, they will make their requirements known to the designers of subject access tools such as the Library of Congress *List of Subject Headings*, the ERIC Thesaurus, and the AAT (Art and Architecture Thesaurus).

Technical services staff in libraries, vocal in the user groups of bibliographic utilities, will begin to pass on the requirements expressed by their compatriots, the reference staff, who are beginning to be quite vocal about the shortcomings of traditional subject access tools.

These inter-relationships will eventually result in the reorganization of library staffs along more functional lines. This in turn will bring about a more representative staff of players in network developments and in national efforts to revise the professional standards for subject access and the like.

Bundy and Wasserman quoted a paper by John Walton[12] in their 1968 paper, and it is a good concluding remark for this paper as well:

> The role of a library is to find that precise balance which introduces only enough routine to keep order and record-keeping integrity, but not so much as to impair the opportunity to afford clientele convenient and unhampered access to resources.

The *library* exists as a system because its staff works in unison to reach the goals of the library. The *library profession* can provide a unitary focus on those goals and can facilitate any group effort which can be marshalled to shift and sway opinion and revise procedures and tools thereby creating a clearer channel for attaining those expressed goals. Maybe the next preconference (in 1988?) will be co-sponsored by RTSD and RASD and the bifurcated nature of the library world will be a thing of the past.

REFERENCES

1. Susan K. Martin and Brett Butler. *Library Automation: The State of the Art II.* Papers presented at the Preconference Institute held at Las Vegas, Nevada, June 22-23, 1973. Chicago, American Library Association, 1975. 191p.

2. Pauline A. Cochrane, "A Paradigm Shift in Library Science," *Information Technology and Libraries*, 2 (March 1983), 3-4.

3. Robert Presthus. *Technological Change and Occupational Response: A Study of Librarians.* Final Report, Project No. 07-1084. Washington, D.C., Office of Education, Bureau of Research, 1970.

4. Philip H. Ennis, "Technological Change and the Professions: Neither Luddite nor Technocrat," *Library Quarterly*, 32 (July 1962), 189-98.

5. Pauline Atherton, compiler and editor. *Handbook for Information Systems and Services.* Paris, Unesco, 1977. p. 59-60.

6. Larry Besant. *American Libraries*, 107 (March 1982), 160.

7. Davis B. McCarn, compiler and editor. *Online Catalogs: Requirements, Characteristics and Costs.* Washington, D.C., Council on Library Resources, 1982. pp. 75-132.

8. Karen Markey, "Online Public Access Catalogs: Users' Problems and Needs," (preprint, 1983).

9. Charles Hildreth. *Online Public Access Catalogs: The User Interface.* Dublin, Ohio, OCLC, 1982.

10. Mary Lee Bundy, "Automation as Innovation," *Drexel Library Quarterly*, 4 (January 1968), 100-108.

11. Carol Mandel. *Subject Access in the Online Catalog.* Washington, D.C., Council on Library Resources, August 1981.

12. John Walton, "The Administration of Libraries," *Johns Hopkins University Ex Libris.* November 1957.

The Ecumenical Library

Michael Gorman

INTRODUCTION

The author of this paper is Director of General Services at the Library of the University of Illinois at Urbana-Champaign—the largest library of a state institution in the United States. The change in organizational structure which he proposes is a model which is the basis for the continuing reorganization of that library. That change, which is intended to be substantially completed by the Spring of 1984, consists of a decentralizing of the professional aspects of original cataloguing and subject bibliography accompanied by a centralizing of all general services including the non-professional aspects of copy cataloguing. The structure of the University of Illinois Library will then, in outline be:

General Services

—Acquisitions
—Copy cataloguing
—Automated records management
—Central Circulation
—Central Reference Services (including the Reference Library, Information Desk, Documents Library)
—Special Collections Libraries
—Area Studies Libraries and Bibliographers
—Bookstacks Management
—Binding

Michael Gorman is Director of General Services at the University Library, University of Illinois, Urbana.

Public Services

More than 35 departmental libraries and an Undergraduate Library, with responsibility for materials selection, reference services, original cataloguing, bibliographic instruction, bibliographic services in their subject, etc., area.

* * * * *

To many librarians it seems as though there is some divinely ordained difference between the two "kinds" of librarianship—technical services and public services. The first is concerned with esoteric "technical" matters and, populated by reclusive adepts, has concerns which are mysterious and methods which are suspect. The second is concerned with "The Public" and, populated by bluff men and women (democrats all), deals with real issues, real people, the library user red in tooth and claw. The methods of public services are perceived as straightforward, practical, empirical, and populist. This dream world division of librarianship is prevalent and, alas, potent. It is reminiscent of the world views that animated the religious strife of seventeenth and eighteenth century Europe. On the one hand, we have the papists and Jesuits of the hidden and hieratic world of technical services, and on the other hand, the Presbyterians and Roundheads of public services serving the public weal. I wish in this paper to propose a different view of librarianship, one which concentrates on similarities not divisions, one devoted to wholeness and to ecumenism.

It is a truism that the main practical forces on modern librarianship are those of economics and automation. As with all truisms, this may be boring but is, nonetheless, true. All libraries have to some extent had to do more with less and have, at least, considered, as a main means to that end, the use of automation. One ironic and most unfortunate result of these forces has been an intensification of the divisions between the two "kinds" of librarianship. In a way, technical services has been where the action is and this has created a feeling of unease and isolation among reference librarians and others in public services. For easily understood evidence of this phenomenon one only has to look at the widening gap between journals devoted to automation/technical services matters and those devoted to public services matters. These days, each of these types of journal is barely comprehensible to those on the other "side."

Economic hardship should bring us together, but all too often has been divisive. Automation should be a unifying and integrating force, but in all too many cases has become the preserve of one "side," a force which has been the plaything of some and the bogeyman of others.

In addition to the need to respond to economic conditions and to take advantage of automation, there is another general force in society—the need to meet the universal demand for more job satisfaction and for self realization at all levels of occupation. The system I am to propose and to specify in some detail meets this humane and necessary component of library administration.

The broad proposal is easily put. It is that we should work, in a systematic and scheduled manner, to abolish the division between technical and public services and to create structures in which groups of librarians are defined not by which aspect of professional librarianship they practice (cataloguing, reference work, etc.) but by the area of service in which they exercise their skills across the whole range of professional librarianship. That is, instead of being limited by the use of one skill or one group of skills, the librarian in this model will be limited only by the type of library user which they serve. In a small library that type might include all users of the library and, in some senses, the model already operates; in a larger library, the type of library user might be defined by subject (e.g., Humanities, Law), by age or educational level (e.g., children, undergraduates), by area (e.g., Latin American studies), or by any other characteristic of division which is appropriate to the mission of the library.

Within these areas of service, professional librarians will perform all the tasks that are truly professional. These include selection of materials, collection development, original cataloguing, reference work, bibliographic instruction, and bibliographic services. Each of these tasks will contribute to and inform each other. A necessary precondition of this proposal is a careful analysis of what constitutes the professional quantum of each task. As traditionally defined, each aspect of library work contains elements of non-professional work, which elements tend to predominate over the professional elements. This simple fact often leads to a misuse of human resources and to feelings of job dissatisfaction.

A simple diagram of the way in which traditional libraries are organized can be seen in Figure 1 in which the library is divided vertically into two main divisions, and each is further subdivided

Figure 1

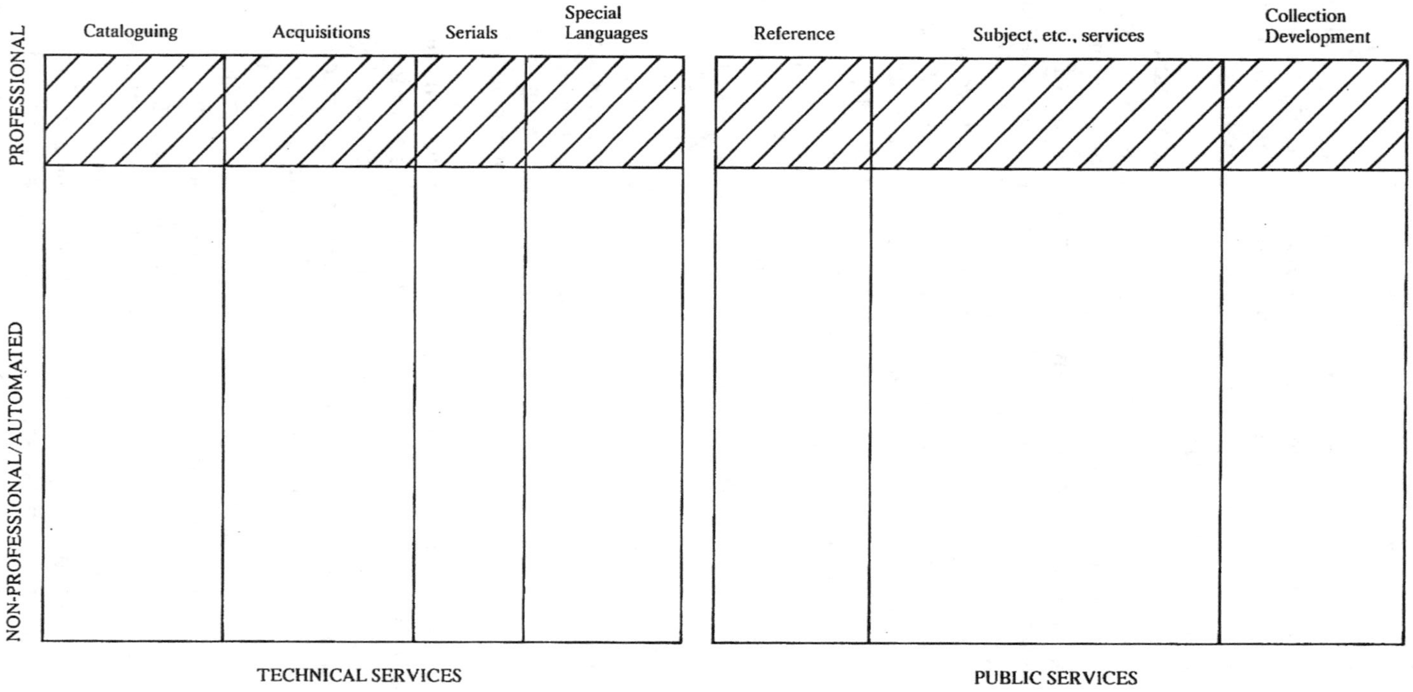

	PROFESSIONAL	NON-PROFESSIONAL/AUTOMATED
Cataloguing		
Acquisitions		
Serials		
Special Languages		

TECHNICAL SERVICES

	PROFESSIONAL	NON-PROFESSIONAL/AUTOMATED
Reference		
Subject, etc., services		
Collection Development		

PUBLIC SERVICES

vertically into specialized task areas. The shaded area in each subdivision represents the quotient of professional tasks.

I propose in place of this a horizontal division as in Figure 2 in which the main professional division is subdivided horizontally, and where the subdivisions numbered 1–n represent the various categories of library user towards which the total professional efforts of a group of librarians are directed. In the lower block, most of the vertical subdivisions seen in the first diagram are retained, though modified and redefined somewhat as set out in more detail below. Fundamentally, the proposed organization depends upon an analysis of professional tasks and a regrouping based not on the particular technical skill deployed but upon categories of library user.

To illustrate this analysis and regrouping I shall take each of the commonly found skill divisions of librarianship and record what, in my opinion, constitutes the professional and the clerical/automated aspects of that division. Although the proportion of professional tasks in each group varies, a basic assumption is that there is always at least 60 percent (and usually a higher percentage) of any broad category of library activity which can be carried out by non-professional workers and/or by machines.

Cataloguing is, perhaps, the task in which the professional/non-professional division can most clearly be seen and which can most easily be restructured. With the widespread use of copy cataloguing, most notably through OCLC, even the largest library user can derive 80 percent or more of its cataloguing records from other libraries. Smaller libraries have recorded "hit rates" that approach 100 percent. Copy cataloguing is not a professional function. This is not to say that it does not require skills, but simply that those skills are not of a professional nature. A very high volume of cataloguing can be achieved by the use of trained clerical workers, the intensive use of terminals, and practical and efficient organization of workflow. Devices such as clear guidelines to the clerical staff and the delegation of decision making to the lowest level at which it can be efficiently carried out will ensure that the traditional, and traditionally inefficient, cataloguing department can largely be replaced by a speedier and more cost effective copy cataloguing operation. There still remains, of course, the less than 20 percent of the materials acquired which need original cataloguing. In most general libraries a simple reduction of the professional cataloguing staff to reflect the proportion of original cataloguing (e.g., from 15 to 3, 10 to 2, 5 to 1) will not work because the range of subjects and

Figure 2

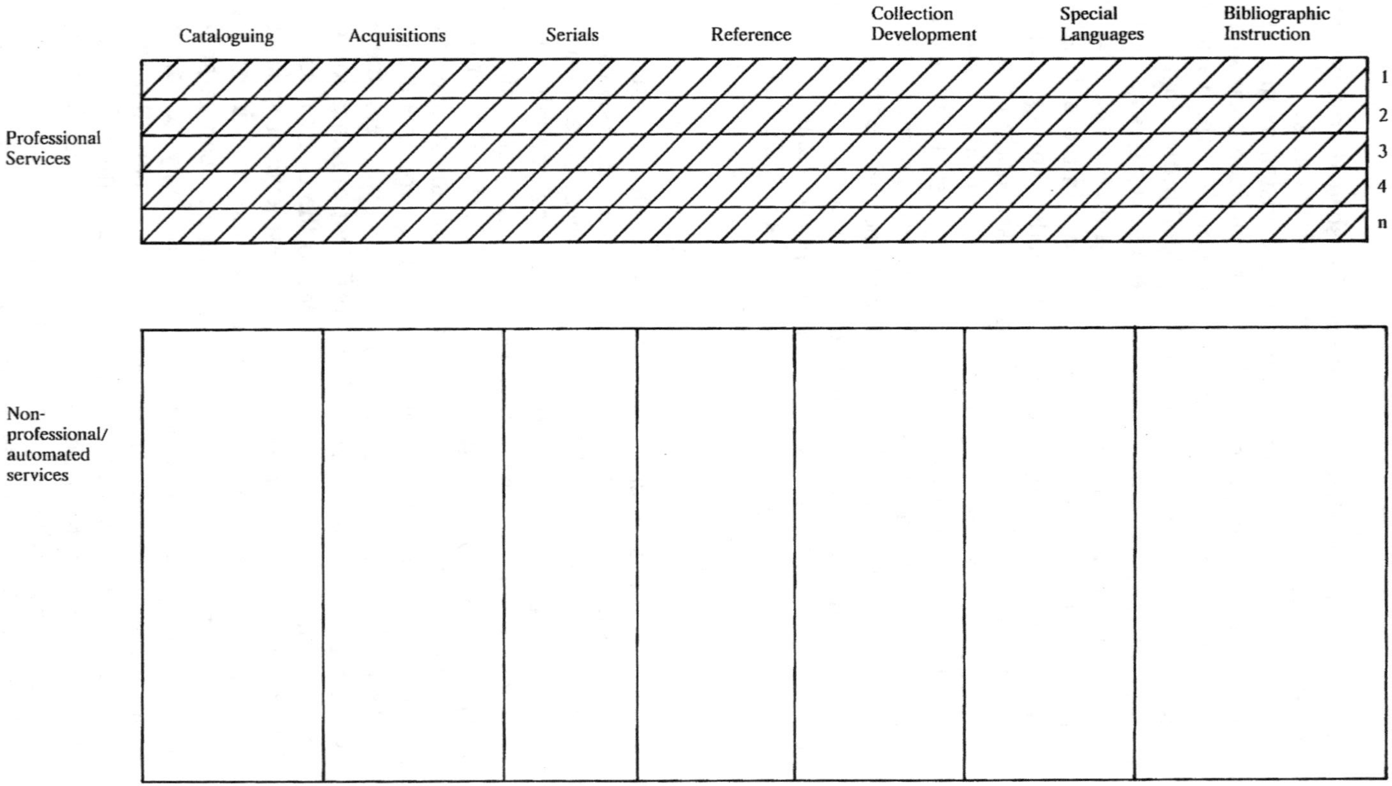

	Cataloguing	Acquisitions	Serials	Reference	Collection Development	Special Languages	Bibliographic Instruction
1							
2							
3							
4							
n							

Professional Services

Non-professional/automated services

languages which need to be covered will be as broad as it was before and it is exceedingly unlikely that such small groups will be able to deal with that range. What is needed is not massive reduction but redeployment, not a cut of 80 percent of the cataloguing staff but a smaller reduction (almost inevitable because of the need to pay for the copy cataloguing operation) of, say, from 15 to 10—those ten persons to spend, say, 25% of their time cataloguing. The remainder of their time will have to be allotted to other professional tasks.

Acquisitions work is an area with a very high proportion of clerical and automated (or automatable) tasks. The basic functions of ordering, claiming, and receipt can be carried out entirely by non-professional staff. Experience over the years in our Library (at the University of Illinois at Urbana-Champaign) has shown that fewer than 10 percent of orders need extensive bibliographic searching of the kind that requires professional librarians. Acquisitions accounting is a high level task but not one that is suited to, or requires, professional library skills. The organization of acquisitions, setting up and monitoring of approval and blanket order plans, dealing with book suppliers and other materials vendors may all, to a greater or lesser extent, need the attention of professional librarians. On the side of acquisitions work that deals with collection development, management, and evaluation, and with budget allocation and reallocation, there is, of course, much for professional librarians to do. I would contend that, even in the largest library, these activities would not require a large number of full-time equivalent librarians, and that those activities can, and should, be divorced from the clerical/automated aspects of acquisitions.

Circulation is a wholly clerical/automated activity. The role of the professional librarian is limited to defining circulation policy and to the construction of organizations and systems in which that policy can be carried out efficiently and fairly. This distinction can be carried over into the subject of the construction and maintenance of automated systems. It is imperative that professional librarians specify the aims and the content of such systems, that they devise the policies for the use of automated systems, and that they monitor the performance of the operating systems. Such functions as data base maintenance and the operation of automated systems are clearly clerical in nature.

The general reference function has traditionally been carried out by groups which are preponderantly professional. Reference work has been seen as a valid province for professional skills. Economic considerations and questions of efficient use of human resources may well produce a reconsideration of this point of view, one which will, at least, consider the possibility of distinguishing between different kinds of demands made on reference services. Those distinctions will, I believe, reveal a similar breakdown as between professional and clerical functions, in the same proportions, seen in looking at other aspects of library work. In all the currently fashionable blether about "information based societies," "the information age," and the dominance of information science in library education and research, there lies one important truth. It is not that libraries are primarily about information transfer or that information is qualitatively more important than the knowledge and culture which form the true basis of the library's mission. The truth is that information is quantitatively the predominant commodity with which most libraries deal. In looking at the whole spectrum of demands upon reference service, we find directional questions, procedural questions, catalogue information, and simple factual questions to be in the majority. Given this, it is clear that establishing a non-professionally staffed information desk will draw off this class of demand and leave the professional librarians in the general reference setting to concentrate on the higher non-informational service which they are uniquely qualified to give. Such a move will involve strategies as to the placing of, and distinction between, the two service points, will involve the creation of a core reference collection of informational materials, and will involve (as will all aspects of this proposal) a reconsideration and reorientation of all staff.

Bibliographic instruction is a curious sub-division of librarianship in that its aims are familiar and longstanding—the imparting of information about the library and its use—but its methods, and the codifications of those methods, are for the most part, of relatively recent vintage. Further, the techniques and the tools which bibliographic instruction is devoted to teaching are themselves changing rapidly. Some of these changes make libraries and their subsystems so easy to use that no bibliographic instruction is necessary. Despite all this, the aims of bibliographic instruction are important and enduring. The role of the professional librarian in bibliographic instruction should consist of devising instructional programs and delivering lectures and other forms of direct instruction. Other devices (tours, questionnaires, tests of library knowledge, etc.) can be left to the non-professional staff.

In all the above analyses, I have deliberately ignored the role of the library paraprofessional. The reason for this is that paraprofessionals have two basic roles—one lies in assisting professionals, the other in acting as the senior member of, or mentor to, fundamentally non-professional groups. Depending upon which role is being played, paraprofessionals will fall logically into the professional block or the clerical/automated group.

With the analysis of each library function completed, the way is open for the restructuring which I propose. At this point, one of the basic forces alluded to at the beginning of this paper—automation—comes into play. The most important aspect of automation in this process is the on-line catalogue (more properly, the on-line bibliographic control system). It is possible to argue that the *raison d'être* of traditional large central technical services departments lies in their access to unique paper files. Proximity to the main catalogue, the serial record, the authority file, the on-order file, the binding file, etc., etc., has been a *sine qua non* for centralized cataloguing, acquisitions, and serials departments. In the online bibliographic control system of the future all the information contained in those files will be available wherever there is a terminal. This means that all kinds of professional and non-professional processing work can be carried out in a variety of locations throughout the library, with automation acting as a decentralizing force in allowing the dissolution of the massive centralized processing departments of the past.

Given an online bibliographic system and a categorization of professional tasks, the way is open for professional/non-professional regrouping. I have mentioned the psychological element of such a drastic reorientation before. This may be as important as the training/retraining element. It is not enough to teach a cataloguer the elements of reference service or to teach a reference librarian the mysteries of cataloguing codes and classification schemes. Beyond these, one needs a commitment to, and understanding of, parts of librarianship which may be new, and even inimical, to the ex-cataloguer or ex-reference librarian. Thus the educational process in creating the new structure is both important and complex. The planning for this transfer of responsibilities needs, as do all such plans, detailed statistical information and intensive educational and orientation programmes.

The re-grouping of professional librarians around subject and other user categories will not only bring better services to the library users they serve, it will also produce more job satisfaction and more career potential for the librarians involved. We will see an intensification of professionalism as each aspect of the practice of librarianship is brought to bear on the range of library service. The concentration of nonprofessional/automated activities in the center of the library will have similarly favourable results. With such concentration come economies of scale and higher productivity together with a uniformity of application of policies. Not only will the librarians be more professional and receive more satisfaction in their work, but also new career opportunities will open for library clerical staff. There will be a restoration of dignity to non-professional library work as each type of library worker will understand their work and their role within the library more clearly.

Contrary to the impression of many, these are good times to be a librarian. Economics and automation are forcing drastic reconsiderations of procedures and structures. These reassessments can be painful, can challenge deepseated beliefs and prejudices; they can also liberate. In bringing together the two "kinds" of librarians, we shall be reacting in a positive manner to these pressures and will allow a new wholeness and new dimensions of library service in the ecumenical library of the future.

Noblesse Oblige: Collection Development as a Public Service Responsibility

Larry Earl Bone

It may seem ironic for one who has been invited to submit an article to a journal issue concerned with the technical services contribution to reference librarianship to take issue with the technical services sector, somewhat like the guest at a dinner party criticizing the other invitees.

In actual fact, the author of this article is taking issue not so much with the technical services area but rather with the public service one which very recently seems to be abdicating its responsibility for an important activity—that of collection development.

The Godden, Fachan, and Smith 1982 bibliography on collection development and acquisitions[1] and Thomas Nisonger's helpful one on collection evaluation[2] would suggest that there is a growing interest in having technical services play a leadership role in the development of collections. Moreover, the recent sponsorship of institutes on collection development by the Resources and Technical Services Division of ALA in various sections of the country reflects the technical service sector's attitude that collection development is its rightful province. It is this Division, furthermore, which has published a guide for collection developers.[3] Rather than carp at such activity, perhaps one should be grateful that some group is taking the initiative in collection development which, relatively speaking, has not received such intensive interest in the past. Why this author regards it as the wrong group, he will strive to answer in this brief article.

The history of technical services will show, as Helen Tuttle

Larry Earl Bone is Director of Libraries and Professor, Mercy College, Westchester County, New York. He is also formerly President of ALA's Reference and Adult Services Division. This article was written when he served as Visiting Professor, Peabody College, Vanderbilt University, Nashville, Tennessee.

© 1984 by The Haworth Press, Inc. All rights reserved.

pointed out several years ago in her masterful overview of the development of technical services during the last one hundred years, a primary concern with the areas of cataloging and classification, first, then acquisitions, serials, and binding later, and at one point circulation.[4] Collection development, not really acknowledged as an area in its own right for many years, she observed, "once it ceased to be selection has floated cheerfully between the technical and reader services, sometimes attaining the dignity of an independent unit of its own."[5] The "floating" has not always had a clear course, however, as Stanley McElderberry showed in his review of public services activity in collection development in academic libraries during the same one hundred year period.[6]

One can understand the ambiguity when one acknowledges that technical services as a separate entity is itself a development less than fifty years old. In the early days of the modern library movement no distinction was made between "technical" and "public" service, nor had these modifiers yet entered library terminology. The primary responsibilities of acquiring books and then cataloging and classifying them seemed to be enough for librarians to handle in the earliest stages of library development and the areas to which the greatest energies were directed. These responsibilities were most clearly reflected in the concerns of librarians in the period from 1876 to 1900. Reference service, as American library history shows, did not really take form until the last decade of the nineteenth century and even after that developed very slowly in many libraries. Poole's discussion of the selection of materials or of collection development consumed only three pages in his treatment of the management of public libraries in the monumental 1876 report on *Public Libraries in the United States*,[7] and Otis H. Robinson, in the same report, touched on it only obliquely in his discussion of college library administration of the day.[8] That small degree of concern for collection development in the minds of librarians of the day no doubt was a reflection of an attitude that collection development was more of an ancillary process.

Twenty-five years ago, in one of my initial appointments as a director of a small public library in Ohio, I had an experience which helped me begin to put into perspective the rightful place of selection and collection development. This was in the period of the late fifties when libraries of all sizes in the U.S. were expanding. From the first day, I began to receive regularly visits from book salesmen, publishers' representatives, and bookbinders. While the promotion of books through traveling representatives had been a practice for years, the affluent fifties and sixties saw an even greater deployment by publishers and wholesalers of traveling representatives to help libraries spend their institutions' money. This "on the road" ritual quickly caught hold in small libraries and, while in the larger libraries the representatives called on the acquisitions librarians, in the smaller libraries it was the directors whom they sought out. Most of the librarians subscribed to the reviewing sources, but they, as I, it is probable, found that making acquaintances with some of these salespeople was a welcome relief from the multitude of responsibilities which came with small library administration and a valuable source of information about publishing activity.

There was a great variety among these individuals. Some were neophyte salesmen with sweating palms hoping to persuade the librarian to purchase their wares and thereby help them prove their sales prowess; others brought their wives so that one could "get to know the family," but there were others who were keenly interested in helping librarians of small libraries with their selection and collection development. There was a real assortment among these salespeople, and needless to say, not all were especially erudite. Later many such representatives were sent out to promote publishers' remainders but this was not generally true at that time. These salespeople had information about books and publishing activities of the day which frequently proved helpful to the librarian.

I remember especially, out of all of those individuals, an elderly Scribner representative who was responsible for promoting the Scribner reference book line. He was a very courtly gentleman, a bookish person of another generation, who regarded his occupation as a high calling. I suspect that his breed of book salespeople is a vanishing lot, and that, in fact, the traveling representatives to libraries as a means of disseminating information about books may be soon regarded as a quaint custom of the past.

My conversations with the Scribner representative were always on a particularly civilized level. We talked about books and libraries and on more than one occasion he made the observation that, in his opinion, the best libraries were ones whose collections were carefully built by librarians knowledgeable of both the quality of books and of their communities' needs. At the end of our conversations he might mention a Scribner volume or set which he thought would increase the quality of a reference collection, but he never used high pressure tactics. On one of his initial visits, when I responded that I thought that I should include the order librarian in the discussion, he asked gently, "Don't you think that the reference librarian might be another good judge?" I think that in his own courteous way he was saying that the reference librarian was probably the *best* judge.

As you can tell from my remembering this individual after so many years, I respected his approach and his awareness of the two underlying principles of book selection and collection development—quality and user need. I believe, moreover, that he perceived that those individuals at the reference or information desk should be the ones most aware of the collection's ability to serve those user needs. I agreed with him then and I agree with that proposition today.

I use this small story from my past to underscore the basic thesis of this article—that public service librarians are indeed the most logical agents in the collection development process—and to place into context the role of collection development in public service.

I would be remiss if I did not admit here that, aside from administration, the larger part of my professional experience and activity has been in two principal areas, reference service and collection development. These two areas, from my standpoint, have always seemed to me to be at the heart of librarianship and to be the most fulfilling; they seem also to have an obvious connection.

It should be pointed out quickly that the above is not said to denigrate the efforts and contributions of technical services librarians, for, as the other articles in this issue will surely attest, our libraries could not operate without these efforts. The solid contributions which technical service librarians have made to librarianship and in support of public service have been enormous. Any administrator of a library program, as well as any librarian responsible for public services, must be truly grateful for these contributions.

I would submit, however, that the basic concerns of these two sectors of librarianship sometimes vary considerably. Those who choose the separate paths for their careers frequently have different interests, although, of course, sometimes those who planned careers in public service become more interested in technical services and vice versa. More often, however, there is a basically different orientation between those in technical service and those in the public service sector, reflecting, I believe, their separate concerns or in some cases their differences in temperament.

Public service librarians frequently accuse the technical service personnel of being so involved in routine as to be unconcerned with getting the materials to the shelves expeditiously. They point to the Library of Congress *Subject Headings* as an example of a technical service activity which has produced headings unresponsive to patron terminology, or to AACR2 and the frustrations it has caused library users. Technical service personnel, on the other hand, frequently regard public service personnel as being so unstructured and unsystematic and so unrealistic in their expectations as to be lacking in an understanding of the necessity for attention to detail and of the importance of bibliographic uniformity. Both accusations are, of course, unfair.

The lack of articulation between technical and public services that began to develop in this century and that has subsequently increased has been the concern of many librarians through the years, and attempts have been made in this country and others to bring a closer working relationship. Some thirty years ago Frank Lundy, then director of the University of Nebraska Library, reported his efforts to bring the two areas closer together with his practice of requiring technical service personnel to spend some of their work week in service at the reference desk.[9] Lundy believed that through such assignments technical service personnel could become more sensitive to the ways that users seek information, and access to it, through the public catalog. He believed additionally that such an arrangement created a better understanding between the technical and public service areas.

Such a philosophy may have been at work in French academic libraries when, during the 1960s, as Deputy Librarian of the American Library in Paris, France, I did an informal study of the organization of the university libraries in Paris. In these libraries, personnel assigned to particular subject areas carried out all of the activities related to materials in their subject areas—collection development, acquisitions, cataloging, and reference service. While such organization seemed a reasonable one in many ways, my superficial judgment was that direct reference service suffered as a result of this organization. Insufficient staffing seemed to result in the technical responsibilities receiving more attention.

In spite of Frank Lundy's convincing argument for mixing public and technical service personnel, the idea really never took hold in other large academic libraries. Many such libraries, while perhaps agreeing with this idea in principle, may have found such arrangements impracticable. Moreover, while many American librarians might find the French approach interesting in theory, reorganization for such purposes has never taken place, except perhaps in the smallest American libraries.

One can easily understand that the practice of separating the library's public service and technical service functions, prevalent in the last fifty years, is most logical from a management standpoint, even if one acknowledges the aforementioned inherent problems of such separation. Because American libraries in recent years have developed so highly their reference service and have promoted it through intensive library instruction programs, it is perhaps understandable that collection development has not always been viewed as an essential component of public service. Anyone who observes the extremely active reference service of many large and medium-sized academic and public libraries today will acknowledge that, even now, without some basic restructuring, the reference desk service, like that in the French libraries I observed, could suffer if the same personnel had responsibility for collection development. In more than one academic library that I have visited in recent years, reference librarians performing other behind-the-scenes responsibilities (which some seem to prefer) have had to be sought out by the students or faculty needing assistance. The activity they choose to sacrifice is frequently the most important one of reader assistance. These librarians assume, one would suppose, as did those librarians of the late nineteenth century, that if the library is well organized, the user can somehow find what he wants!

Even when acknowledging the problems, nevertheless, one can easily see, as did the Scribner salesman, that it is at the information desk that the library user is brought into contact with the library's collection and with its strengths and deficiencies. While technical service personnel can provide effectively the support service necessary to acquire and organize the collections, public service librarians who are in daily contact with the library users are undoubtedly most aware of the strengths and weaknesses of the collection.

The establishment of bibliographers and, subsequently, collection development offices in research libraries in recent years separate from public services may be justified on the basis of library size and organization. The *Library Trends* issue of 1966 on the building of university library collections proved, however, if proof were required, that many of our most important university library collections were built in days when separate offices for collection development were not the norm.[10]

Similarly, some of the older established public libraries such as those in New York, Baltimore, Boston, Cleveland, Detroit, and Los Angeles had their fine collections developed by subject-oriented reference personnel. Other emerging urban public libraries, such as those in Cincinnati, Dallas, Denver, Houston, Memphis, and Minneapolis have followed this pattern. Bone and Raines in the early 1970s, in fact, made a case for subject department personnel in large public libraries becoming true subject specialists cognizant of the bibliography of their fields in order that they could become more skilled as reference librarians and more effective as collection builders.[11]

It is not necessary, of course, for every library to be large or subject departmentalized in order to develop public service staff who are knowledgeable in the bibliography of a subject or take an interest in collection development. Peyton Hurt, over thirty-five years ago, suggested methods by which special subject bibliographic knowledge could be developed in the small or medium-sized library.[12] George Bonn's article of the 1970s in which he surveyed collection evaluation techniques—the most comprehensive review of evaluation techniques used at that time—provides assistance for anyone engaged in public service activities who wish to develop such skills.[13] Stueart and Miller, additionally, have recently provided a remarkably well organized treatment of the overall principles and components of present day collection development and instructions for the construction of meaningful collection development policies.[14] Any study of the bibliography of various fields, of collection evaluation techniques, and of systematic examinations of the library's collection will, among other collection development activities, most certainly enhance such public service programs as reference service and library instruction.

Reference and subject departments in any well-run library keep careful records of requests that are unfilled and of those materials for which interlibrary loan is necessary. Such information is invaluable for collection development purposes. Public service librarians and not technical service ones, moreover, are the ones most engaged in community analysis in order to determine the community's stated and unstated needs and should, therefore, be in the best position to evaluate the collection in terms of those needs. The public service activity in community analysis in public libraries, especially during the last thirty years, is a matter of record. It has become the cornerstone of the Public Library Association's Planning Process. James Govan has affirmed the importance of community analysis in the academic setting as well, especially in matching the users and the curriculum to collection needs.[15]

The many public libraries that already view collection development as a public service activity would be unwise to change their patterns in this respect. These libraries, while certainly allocating public service staff time to it, have not found it necessary to include it in its technical support activities. Some academic libraries have retained collection development as a public service endeavor also. Others, I believe, would be wise to follow such organization, not from the standpoint of territorial prerogative, but from that of the logical relationship of activities.

It would be idle, of course, to suggest that the incorporation of the collection development process into the public service responsibilities can succeed without adequate personnel and without adequate administrative support. Collection development, if effective in its execution, takes considerable staff time and effort and other public services should not be robbed to provide the necessary time. Given support, however, the best collection development program can be achieved, I believe firmly, by those involved in direct service to the library's public and will be one of the natural parts of a dynamic public service program.

Finally, I believe that the Scribner salesman was right. Collection development in any library should hold as its basic tenets *quality* and *user need*. Without these considerations any library's service will suffer. With those principles as the touchstone, however, quality collection development will occur and, as an activity, will "float cheerfully" back to public service—which is the rightful and proper domain in which it has always belonged.

REFERENCES

1. Godden, Irene P., Fachan, Karen W., and Smith, Patricia A. *Collection Development and Acquisitions, 1970-1980: An Annotated, Critical Bibliography*. Metuchen, N.J., The Scarecrow Press, 1982.

2. Nisonger, Thomas E. "An Annotated Bibliography of Items Relating to Collection Evaluation in Academic Libraries, 1969-1981." *College and Research Libraries*, 43: 300-311 (July 1982).

3. American Library Association. Collection Development Committee. Resources and Technical Services Division. *Guidelines for Collection Development*. Chicago, American Library Association, 1979.

4. Tuttle, Helen W. "From Cutter to Computer: Technical Services in Academic and Research Libraries, 1876-1976." *College and Research Libraries*, 37: 421-451 (September 1976).

5. Ibid.

6. McElderberry, Stanley. "Readers and Resources: Public Services in Academic and Research Libraries, 1876-1976." *College and Research Libraries*, 37: 408-420.

7. U.S. Bureau of Education. *Public Libraries in the United States of America, Their History, Condition, and Management.* Washington, D.C., U.S. Government Printing Office, 1876, pp. 479-481.

8. Ibid., pp. 505-525.

9. Lundy, Frank K. "Reference vs. Catalog; A Basic Dilemma." *Library Journal*, 80:19-23 (January 1, 1955).

10. "Collection Development in University Libraries." Jerrold Orne, editor. *Library Trends* 15 (October 1966).

11. Bone, Larry Earl and Raines, Thomas. "The Nature of the Urban Main Library: Its Relation to Selection and Collection Building." *Library Trends*, 20: 625-639 (April 1972).

12. Hurt, Peyton. "Staff Specialization: A Possible Substitute for Departmentalization." *ALA Bulletin*, 29: 417- 421 (July 1935).

13. Bonn, George S. "Evaluation of the Collection." *Library Trends*, 22: 265-304 (January 1974).

14. Stueart, Robert D. and Miller, George B., Jr. *Collection Development*. JAI Press, 1980. 2v.

15. Govan, James. "Community Analysis in an Academic Environment." *Library Trends*, 24: 541-555 (January 1974).

DOCUMENT DESCRIPTION

The Impact of AACR2 on the Harvard Library Union Catalog: A Case Study

Carol F. Ishimoto

THE UNION CATALOG

The Harvard University Library is best described as a confederation of nearly a hundred libraries in an administratively decentralized but centrally coordinated organization. It is the oldest library in the United States and ranks as the largest university library in the world with 10.5 million volumes. Organizationally, the ten libraries of the Harvard College Library, generally referred to as the central collections, together with the departmental and special research libraries of the Faculty of Arts and Sciences make up approximately 70% of the total volume count. The remaining 30% is held by the libraries of other Faculties, namely, the Graduate Schools of Business Administration, Design, Divinity, Education, Government, Law, Medicine, and Public Health. Although these libraries have their own catalogs of holdings, their records are contributed to Harvard's Union Catalog, which helps to hold together the confederation that forms the Harvard University Library (HUL).

Today Harvard's Union Catalog exists in two parts: Union Catalog 1, a card catalog, and Union Catalog 2, a microfiche catalog. Union Catalog 1 is the original Union Catalog which Professor Ar-

---

Carol F. Ishimoto, a Librarian on the staff of the Harvard University Libraries, is editor of the Library's union catalog.

© 1984 by The Haworth Press, Inc. All rights reserved.

chibald Cary Coolidge, Director of the Harvard University Library (1910–1928), was largely responsible for building up during his administration. The Widener Library, which was completed in 1915 has housed the Union Catalog ever since. This is primarily an author or main entry catalog, excluding works in non-Roman scripts such as Arabic, Persian, Hebrew, Yiddish, Chinese, Japanese, and Korean, all of which are found in their separate catalogs. Editing the catalog records contributed by the Harvard libraries has been the responsibility of catalogers in Widener. However, editing has been minimal, limited almost entirely to the collocation of variant forms of names and titles whenever possible to facilitate user access and to avoid unnecessary duplicate purchases. Given the age of the Library, Union Catalog 1, with its nearly 6 million records, represents a variety of local cataloging standards as well as idiosyncratic practices. Nevertheless, scholars and users in general consider it one of the most useful reference tools at Harvard. Union Catalog 1 was closed to the addition ot new records on July 1, 1982 on the assumption that all of the contributing libraries would thereafter be able to produce machine-readable records for Union Catalog 2, the supplement to Union Catalog 1, through a bibliographic utility (OCLC or RLIN) or Harvard's local MARC system.

When Harvard began limited participation in OCLC during the 1970s, one of the long-range applications considered for the machine-readable data produced through the online shared cataloging system was an eventual Union Catalog in microform that could be distributed throughout the decentralized University Library system, including the Dumbarton Oaks Library in Washington, D.C. and the Harvard and Radcliffe house (dormitory) libraries. It should be added that the idea of a distributable Union Catalog at Harvard was not new; in 1939, Thomas Franklin Currier, Assistant Librarian in charge of cataloging and classification in the Harvard College Library (1913–1936) and later Associate Librarian (1937–1940), asked the following questions in his article on "Cataloging and classification at Harvard, 1878–1938":

> Who can forecast the future? Will the student in the year 2038 be concerned only with reading microfilms on which has been gathered for his individual use all that has been printed and written on a given subject? Will the card catalogue itself be on film or will the processes of reproduction and printing be such

that each student may possess, if he so desires, a complete union catalog of books available, these catalogues kept up to date by periodic cumulation?[1]

Planning for the distributable Union Catalog 2 in microform began in November 1978, sixty years ahead of Currier's forecast of the year 2038, when Douglas Bryant, Director of the Harvard University Library, appointed a Union Catalog Planning Committee. The eleven members included a senior member of the Harvard University Office for Information Technology, library administrators, and reference, collection development, catalog, and system librarians. During its deliberations the Planning Committee considered the rationale of a distributable Union Catalog in microform, its characteristics and user-related issues, the services needed to support such a catalog in a decentralized organization, and finally, the systems development work necessary to produce the catalog. No attempt will be made here to describe the planning process, except to say that it was an exceedingly complex undertaking which required the efforts of many librarians during the two and a half years before the first distributable Union Catalog 2 in microfiche, together with microfiche readers, was installed in August 1981 at 130[2] stations in the University Library system. By this time the catalog was officially named the HUL Distributable Union Catalog (DUC). The support, counsel, and wisdom of Professor Oscar Handlin, Director of the Harvard University Library 1979-), should be acknowledged because he is primarily responsible for making the DUC an actuality. He has been instrumental in obtaining funds from the University administration and in convincing the faculty that a new multiple-access catalog for Harvard's decentralized library system can serve them better than the single author entry approach of Union Catalog 1.

The first DUC cumulation of 1,357,000 catalog entries for 362,000 titles was produced from OCLC tapes (largely pre-AACR2) for cataloged items, plus data from the internal acquisitions system for items on order or received but not yet cataloged. The catalog is divided into author/title and subject catalogs containing the Library of Congress and National Library of Medicine headings in two alphabets. The DUC is not a register/index catalog; instead, the entries are alphabetically arranged with full bibliographic records under author or other type of main entry and briefer entries under other access points, such as title, joint author, series, and subject. The alphabetic arrangement with full bibliographic record under the main entry was strongly recommended by reference, collection development, and catalog librarians to avoid the double look-up that a register/index approach necessitates when a full bibliographic record is needed. While the two-step process of the register/index might not be necessary in many of the Harvard libraries or for the general users, frequent consultation of the full bibliographic record is required by the staff and by much of the research that depends on the central research collection of Widener.

In addition to monographs and serials, including those in microform, the DUC includes musical scores, sound recordings, motion pictures, film strips, slide sets, and machine-readable data files. The last four categories are new to the Harvard Union Catalog. Like Union Catalog 1, the non-Roman scripts of the East Asian and Middle Eastern languages are excluded, but only until machine capability for handling them is better developed. Hebrew, on the other hand, is now being romanized by the Judaica Department, and the records are being incorporated in the DUC through Harvard's local MARC system.

The author/title catalog of the DUC is recumulated semiannually with monthly cumulated supplements. The subject catalog has semiannual cumulations only. The fifth DUC cumulation, scheduled for September 1983, will have an estimated 2.2 million catalog entries for about 565,000 titles produced from the source files of OCLC, RLIN, Harvard's local MARC and local acquisitions systems, and the Library of Congress/Harvard cooperative MARC project.

THE DUC STANDARDS

A Subcommittee on Bibliographic Standards was appointed in 1978 at the same time as the Union Catalog Planning Committee. The Subcommittee's primary charge was to formulate a Harvard University Library bibliographic standard to be followed by all the libraries producing records for the Distributable Union Catalog. Given the traditional autonomous status of the Harvard Libraries, based on a system of financing that has often been characterized as "each tub on its own bottom," the imposition of standardized cataloging practices necessitated by the automated DUC (on microfiche) was a radical change. Difficulties of enforcement could be anticipated; but the visibility of a unit's cataloging in the DUC has encouraged standardization in form of entry and bibliographic description used throughout the University Library system. It is understood that the extent of the DUC's usefulness for the users as well as in the public services, collection development, and cataloging activities is determined by the quality of the data base.

The Harvard University Library Bibliographic Standards incorporate the following as the standards for the DUC:

1. AACR2 as interpreted by the Library of Congress for the choice and form of entry, the bibliographic description, and the establishment of name authorities;
2. the CONSER standard for the cataloging of serials;
3. the Library of Congress and the National Library of Medicine subject heading systems for subject analysis; and,
4. the Library of Congress MARC conventions as implemented by OCLC and RLIN for machine encoding.

To assist in maintaining the Bibliographic Standards for the DUC, there are three centralized services: the Harvard University Library Union Catalog Services Office, the Harvard University Library CONSER Office, and the Harvard College Library/Faculty of Arts and Sciences Cataloging Support Services.

The primary function of the Union Catalog Services Office (UCSO), established in 1980, is to produce a consistent and standardized DUC. This is a complex and difficult task. UCSO interprets and communicates policy related to the Bibliographic Standards, monitors decentralized cataloging in the University Library system, resolves bibliographic problems related to quality control such as discrepancies in form of headings, creates cross-references by means of encoding and keying authority records submitted by libraries, eliminates duplicate records, and produces a master record by a compositing process when more than one library has cataloged the same work. Human review of all the bibliographic records contributed to the DUC is impossible; therefore, UCSO tries to maintain a consistent catalog by instruction and corrective training of cataloging staff in the use of the Bibliographic Standards. The result has been a shared responsibility by UCSO and all cataloging units for the maintenance of the DUC, in contrast to the maintenance of Union Catalog 1, which has been the sole responsibility of the library (Widener) that houses it.

Although the Harvard University Library CONSER Office has

existed since the late seventies when Harvard became a CONSER participant, its responsibilities increased as a result of the DUC. The Office provides serial cataloging services for many libraries which are without professional catalogers and does the terminal work of claiming or inputting CONSER records to the CONSER data base for the Harvard University Library. Harvard participates in the Library of Congress NACO (Name Authorities Cooperative) Project, and the CONSER Office is also responsible for coordinating this activity. To promote standardization of serial cataloging for the DUC, workshops are conducted for instruction in and interpretation of AACR2.

The Harvard College Library/Faculty of Arts and Sciences Cataloging Support Services (CSS) was established in 1981 to provide monograph cataloging services, including OCLC input, for many small libraries lacking the cataloging expertise that would enable them to contribute to the DUC. For the libraries with professional cataloging staffs, but with no access to OCLC, CSS provides centralized terminal input for records. The services provided by CSS have contributed substantially to standardization of the DUC.

In the fall of 1980, before the three centralized units mentioned above began to provide their support services for the DUC, the Subcommittee on Bibliographic Standards conducted a series of workshops on AACR2 to train the Harvard technical services staffs in the use of the new cataloging rules as implemented by the Library of Congress. Just what the actual impact of AACR2 would be on the existing local catalogs and the DUC was not fully realized until 1981 when the implementation of the new code began.

THE IMPACT OF AACR2

First, it should be understood that the DUC is not a new catalog started simultaneously with the implementation of AACR2. Initially, the DUC was produced from OCLC tapes which dated back to 1977. Therefore, when the Library of Congress AACR2 forms of headings became the required standard for the DUC with the implementation of the new code of rules in 1981, catalogers were immediately faced with the problem of incompatible headings, and there was no economically feasible means of updating them from the pre-AACR2 headings to AACR2. In the absence of any possible alternative at the time, it was decided to split files between the earlier and later forms of headings as the need for changes was encountered during the cataloging process. To link the split files for the users, the following general see references were prepared:

[The pre-AACR2 form of heading]
This heading has been superseded.
For other materials see under currently established heading:
[AACR2 form of heading]

and

[The AACR2 form of heading]
This is the currently established heading.
For other materials, see: [pre-AACR2 form of heading]

Splitting the works of a given entity is clearly a disservice to users. Not only does it result in a double look-up, but, even more unfortunate, the reference itself may be missed entirely by users, including members of the staff. For instance, there are times when unnecessary duplicate orders are placed because the reference linking the split files is overlooked. In addition, the time spent searching and filling interlibrary loan requests in the central research collection has increased. At any rate, during 1981–1982 more than 3,000 split files were created for the DUC, a time-consuming and expensive task for catalogers and the Union Catalog Services Office.

During the first quarter of 1983 the University Library's Office for Systems Planning and Research mounted an inhouse DUC online maintenance system for updating headings to AACR2 as well as making other corrections. The availability of the system has eliminated the need to establish any more split files. It should not be assumed, however, that the local maintenance capability can readily update all types of DUC pre-AACR2 forms of headings to AACR2. Given the rule changes, the task is not that straightforward. A personal name change from an earlier to a later form is not a problem, but changes in geographic names and headings for corporate bodies can become very complex and laborious recataloging problems because such headings exist in combination with other elements as well as alone. The following examples attempt to illustrate the domino effect of changes resulting from upgrading a geographic name to AACR2:

(1) Change in the form of geographic name:

Pre-AACR2: St. Gall, Switzerland
LC/AACR2: Saint Gall (Switzerland)

(2) Changes triggered from the above change for those corporate bodies formerly entered under St. Gall, Switzerland but now entered directly under their names, such as:

Pre-AACR2: St. Gall, Switzerland (Benedictine abbey)
LC/AACR2: Kloster St. Gallen

Pre-AACR2: St. Gall, Switzerland, Stiftsbibliothek
LC/AACR2: Stiftsbibliothek Sankt Gallen

Pre-AACR2: St. Gall, Switzerland. Hochschule für Wirtschaften- und Sozialwissenschaften
LC/AACR2: Hochschule St. Gallen für Wirtschafts- und Sozialwissenschaften

(3) Changes in series formerly entered under St. Gall, Switzerland but now entered directly under their titles, such as:

Pre-AACR2: St. Gall, Switzerland, Hochschule für Wirtschafts- und Sozialwissenschaften. Veröffentlichungen der Hochschule St. Gallen für Wirtschafts- und Sozialwissenschaften : Schriftenreihe Betriebswirtschaft.

LC/AACR2: Veröffentlichungen der Hochschule St. Gallen
(assumption) für Wirtschafts- und Sozialwissenschaften. Schriftenreihe Betriebswirtschaft.

(4) Changes in the reference structure for the above files have to be reviewed and redone according to AACR2.

In an effort to be consistent with the Library of Congress AACR2 form of established headings, a significant amount of cataloging time is spent searching for variant forms of names, both personal and corporate. Nevertheless, conflicts are unavoidable because the forms of names can vary from publication to publication and many of the rules are subject to different interpretations. It is reasonable to assume that the implementation of AACR2 has been just as difficult for the Library of Congress, considering the extensive number of rule interpretations issued by LC and necessitated by the nature of the code. Based on Harvard's experience in the use of AACR2, a code more dependent on logic and structure in the formation of headings would be less expensive and more efficient to implement because of the difficulties in determining the predominantly used form of names. Such a code would lessen the impact on cataloging productivity, diminishing the backlogs of uncataloged materials which in the end directly affect the users in the library community.

The following examples point out only a few of the types of problems related to variant forms of headings:

(1) Variant forms of name appearing in different works of a current author writing in Spanish:

LC/AACR2: Frutos, Pedro de
Los enigmas del camino de Santiago / Pedro de Frutos. c1977.

but, Harvard's book by the same author: Frutos Garcia, Pedro de
Leyendas gallegas / Pedro de Frutos Garcia. 1980.

Note: This situation existed prior to AACR2, but it was not mandatory in pre-DUC times to conform to LC forms of headings.

(2) Variant forms of a corporate body's name appearing in different publications of the body.

(One particularly troublesome rule is 24.13, type 5, in which an attempt is made to indicate when a subordinate or related body should be entered as a subheading of the parent body and when it should be entered directly under its own name.)

When the title page reads: Matthaei Botanical Gardens of the University of Michigan
the LC/AACR2 form is: University of Michigan, Matthaei Botanical Gardens

but, if the title page reads: Matthaei Botanical Gardens University of Michigan
the LC/AACR2 form is: Matthaei Botanical Gardens

Therefore, the manner in which the heading for the body is established, subordinately or not, will depend on the form of name appearing in the first item cataloged which can vary from library to library.

(2) Variant forms of a personal name in the Cyrillic alphabet and the use of non-systematic or systematic romanization:

The decision by Library of Congress to apply the alternative rule of adopting non-systematic romanization for well-known persons appearing in general English-language reference sources and systematic romanization for those who have yet to become famous has unfortunately caused considerable confusion for both users and staff. The dual standard has also contributed to inconsistencies.

Pre-AACR2:
(systematic romanization)
Mandel'shtam, Osip Emil'evich, 1891–1938

LC/AACR2 (1st version):
(non-systematic romanization)
Mandelstam, Osip Yemilyevich, 1891–1938

LC/AACR2 (revised version):
(systematic romanization)
Mandel'shtam, Osip, 1891–1938

Since this person appears as Mandelstam in the current editions of the Britannica, Americana, and Collier's encyclopedias, the first LC/AACR2 version, using the non-systematic romanization for the name, is theoretically correct. Nevertheless, after consultation with LC, the Slavic catalogers were faced with a second revision of the name to conform with LC.

In addition to problems with variant forms of headings, there are inconsistencies that can occur, particularly for corporate bodies, in the absence of rules which would produce more logically structured headings. The following examples of similar bodies that have been treated differently show how split files may result, to the confusion of users and catalogers alike:

LC/AACR2: All Souls College (University of Oxford)
LC/AACR2: University of Oxford, Corpus Christi College
LC/AACR2: Nauchnyĭ sovet po istorii mirovoĭ kul′tury (Akademiia nauk SSSR)

LC/AACR2: Akademii͡a nauk SSSR. Nauchnyĭ sovet po istoricheskoĭ geografii i kartografii
Note: There are far more intricate examples than these, but space does not permit their inclusion.

Uniform titles will become even more useful when the DUC also becomes accessible as an online catalog and abbreviated records must be used on guide screens. Unfortunately, Chapter 25, which deals with uniform titles, has been revised very little from the first edition of AACR; it fails, for instance, to address the problems which resulted from the introduction of corporate emanation with the consequent increase in title main entries. This, of course, has particularly complicated the work of serial catalogers.

An unfortunate result of the treatment of uniform titles is the amount of research required to determine the uniform title for an author's works. For example, much time can be spent in making the choice between "Works" (for complete works), "Selections," and a specific collective term, such as "Novels," "Poems," or "Short stories," for the *collected works* of a person writing in a particular form.

For Classical and Byzantine Greek works, as well as stories with many versions, the English-language reference sources must be searched first to determine whether a uniform title in English or the vernacular should be chosen. Such a choice in a research library has a tendency to complicate rather than facilitate access because the user can never predict which language is likely to be used for similar works. For instance, Aristotle's Physics has the uniform title *Physics*, but his Metaphysics has the uniform title *Metaphysica*.

For census publications[3] the primary purpose of the uniform title, presumably to bring together materials about the same place, is defeated because of the omission of a geographic qualifier immediately after the uniform title and before the date of the census. Therefore, the census of population publications of the United States, for example, interfile among similar censuses of other countries and are not found in a single file where most users would expect to find them. These are just some of the more critical problems experienced in the application of uniform titles in the DUC.

In April 1983 Harvard's online link to the Library of Congress in connection with the cooperative name authority and cataloging project became operational. The link is particularly advantageous for the DUC because it provides direct online access to LC's name authority file for the most current authority information, thus eliminating the previous time-consuming task of searching the National Union Catalog as well as second-guessing LC.

In conclusion, the substance of a paper on "The objects of cataloging" presented by Professor Archibald Cary Coolidge,[4] former Director of the Harvard University Library, on June 21, 1921, at a meeting of the Catalog Section of the American Library Association, is just as pertinent today, in considering the impact of AACR2, as it was more than sixty years ago. He opened his remarks by saying that his observations were not "based on principles of theoretical perfection, that is to say on unlimited funds." He was looking at cataloging from "the standpoint of a large general library whose books deal with an infinite number of topics and are in many languages, and which has to regard its catalog not as a work of art, but as the best makeshift it can provide with the resources at its disposal. . . . Amidst the continual application of numerous rules, torn between our desire for the utmost service and the urgent need of economy, it is sometimes well to get back to first principles and to ask oneself what the object of it all is. Who are the public we are trying to serve and what do they really need from the catalog?"

In Coolidge's words, "The object of cataloging is to make knowledge available to the public, and, as in the case of writing books, the best results can be attained only by clearness of thought, skillful arrangement and wise restriction. Like an unreadable book, an unworkable catalog fails in its object. . . . On the other hand, a good library catalog. . . renders a very real service to the public and takes an honorable place among the agencies that contribute to the progress of our civilization."

REFERENCES

1. T. Franklin Currier, "Cataloging and Classification at Harvard, 1878-1938," *Harvard Library Notes*, 29:242 (March 1939).
2. The number of sets of the DUC distributed today has increased to 145.
3. *Cataloging Service Bulletin*, 12:29 (Spring, 1981).
4. Archibald C. Coolidge, "The Objects of Cataloging," *The Library Journal*, 46:[735]-739 (September 15, 1921).

Inter-Library Loan as an Unobtrusive Measure of Bibliographic Efficiency

Sally Stevenson
Gwen Deiber

One of the most important functions of technical services departments is to provide reference librarians and users with a catalog containing complete and accurate information on the materials held by the library. The enormous difficulties inherent in providing access points or entries and structuring bibliographic records that will fulfill this function have been amply demonstrated by catalog use studies which have shown that in known item searches between 3% and 34% of all catalog users are unsuccessful in finding items owned by the library and represented in the catalog.[1] While reference librarians and other knowledgeable users of catalogs recognize the necessity of searching alternative entries for items not found by the initial search strategy, others experiencing failure on their first attempt are likely to conclude the library does not own the item. At the State University of New York at Albany (SUNYA) many of the requests submitted to Inter-Library Loan (ILL) are the result of such user failure. Although this fact had been documented for several years, no systematic attempt had been made to analyze the causes of these failures.

Since the implementation of AACR2 in January 1981, however, the ILL staff has observed a sharp increase in the number of patron requests for items owned by the SUNYA Libraries. Prior to AACR2, such requests had averaged 9% of all monograph requests and 7%-8% of all serial requests. By the end of the academic year 1981/82, they had grown to 12.2% of all monographs and 11.5% of all serials and were still increasing. It seemed desirable to determine

---

Sally Stevenson is Head, Inter-Library Loan Office of the State University of New York at Albany, NY 12222. Gwen Deiber is Assistant Head, Inter-Library Loan Office at the same library.

© 1984 by The Haworth Press, Inc. All rights reserved.

what factors might be contributing to this increase. It was felt that an analysis of the failures of the ILL clientele, viewed as a microcosm of the Libraries' users, might provide useful information to the catalogers in assessing the effectiveness of the tools they provide and to reference librarians in understanding how patrons approach known item searches.

From December 1, 1982 through March 31, 1983, the requests for owned items were retained and analyzed, thus creating an unobtrusive measure of the impact of AACR2 and other cataloging decisions on service to patrons and reference librarians as well as identifying other problems encountered by patrons in a large research library. While the findings are not necessarily generalizable to the SUNYA user population as a whole, they do provide some insights as to how one subset of the population (ILL users) has adjusted to AACR2.

A variety of resources are available to faculty and students at SUNYA to assist them in making effective use of the library. An extensive program of library instruction for undergraduates is provided by the Library Instruction Unit which offers courses in general library use as well as courses in specific topics such as government publications and legal materials. Members of the Collection Development Unit are active in providing more advanced instruction to graduate students and faculty. Assistance with specific problems is provided by centralized reference desks at both the main library and its branch during most of the hours the Libraries are open. Additional reference staffing is provided at the main library's Government Publications Unit desk during peak hours. Handouts describing various available services are also prominently displayed.

Access to the cataloged collections of the SUNYA Libraries is provided by a union card catalog at the main library and a departmental catalog at the branch library. On December 31, 1980, these catalogs were "frozen." To cover the interim period between January 1981, and the establishment of an on-line catalog, card sets conforming to AACR2 are produced for all new acquisitions and recataloged items. These cards are temporarily filed in the same drawers housing the "frozen" catalog. The two sections of each drawer are separated by divider cards which read:

> ATTENTION OLD cards filed in back of this divider. NEW cards are in front. MAKE SURE YOU CHECK BOTH!

As a partial alternative to the card catalog, public access terminals are available, enabling the user to search the computerized Library Circulation System (LCS) as a quasi-catalog.

Computer printouts of the Libraries' periodical holdings listed by main entry are available at both campuses. This listing is, however, limited to those periodicals which are shelved in designated periodical stacks and, therefore, excludes those shelved in the reference area or the general stacks.

In addition to the cataloged collections, the Libraries also maintain extensive holdings in government publications and microform collections such as ERIC, NTIS, NCJRS, *Early American Imprints*, the Tamiment Library's *Radical Pamphlet Literature, German Books before 1600*, etc. Access to these collections is provided by printed and/or on-line indexes. However, effective use of these collections does require a knowledge that such a collection exists and that the item sought is likely to be found in it.

During a survey, a total of 3503 interlibrary loan requests were processed. Of these 437 (12.2%) were identified as SUNYA owned items. These requests were analyzed and assigned to one of 20 categories of user error or misunderstanding. Attempts were made when possible to contact these requestors and provide instruction in the use of the catalog. Excluded from the survey are requests immediately identified as SUNYA owned at the time of submission.

Somewhat surprisingly, the single largest category (20.6%) resulted from users who failed to find entries in the periodical printout despite having the correct entry. An additional 9.2% of the errors resulted from an inability to find entries in the card catalog (i.e., the "frozen" catalog) even though the monographs were listed under the entry searched. Several persons (2.3% of the requests) confessed that they had not searched the catalog because of their certainty that the item was not owned by the library. A total of 32% of the errors can thus be attributed to patron ineptness or carelessness rather than the Libraries' failure to supply needed catalog entries.

Technical Services Department policies and/or errors were, however, related to 31.3% of the failures. The implementation of AACR2 and the resulting split in card files between pre- and post-AACR2 sections accounted for 11% of the errors. Very few patrons making this type of error were aware of the double files. For those who were aware, the ambiguity of the explanatory cards (i.e., "new cards," "old cards") apparently did not make it clear that, regardless of publication date, cards for titles added or recataloged after January 1981 are filed in the front. Verbal explanations of the concept of the divided catalog were often difficult for patrons to understand and ILL staff frequently escorted patrons to the catalog to demonstrate the arrangement. This finding tends to confirm Brights' observation that when users are required to consult more than one catalog, they almost always fail to consult the smaller file and inevitably miss material relevant to their search.[2]

AACR2 may, however, tend to reduce another category of user failure. Five percent of the errors were contributed by patrons who searched under generic terms such as *Journal, Proceedings,* or *Transactions* rather than corporate author. The increase in title main entries resulting from AACR2's concept of corporate emanation, together with an increase in title added entry cards, should result in more consistency between catalog entries and patron citations. However, the fact that some serials are entered under title will inevitably compound the difficulties in explaining the necessity of searching corporate authors for journals entered under previous rules.

The study also demonstrated patron reliance on the Libraries' printout for identifying what serials are owned by the Libraries as well as the prevalent misconception that all serials are included. As a result, requests for serials listed only in the card catalog, such as the *Journal of Economic Literature, Philosophical Transactions* of the Royal Society of London, *Advances in Librarianship, Annual Review of Sociology, Dissertation Abstracts* and similar titles are regularly submitted to the ILL office. In this survey, they accounted for 7.3% of the requests for owned items. Thus, cataloging policy decisions which determine whether an item is housed in periodicals (and, therefore, appears on the printout) have a direct impact on whether users find these materials. An additional .7% were for periodicals listed in the card catalog but added too recently to appear on the current printout.

The card catalog at the main library also functions as the on-order file for the University Libraries. Title entry was chosen to expedite filing by clerical support staff. Order slips for books acquired on approval or standing order actually signify that the book has been received in Technical Services and can be retrieved by placing a rush cataloging request with the Circulation Unit. Inquiries as to whether patrons had checked for recent publications under title invariably met with a negative response. This tends to confirm previous studies that have shown that people generally use authors for entry to the catalog and most do not persevere very long in their search.[3] It appears that the structure and function of the on-order aspect of the catalog may not be widely understood. Three percent of the requests were for on-order items and were retrieved from the Cataloging Unit.

Only 5% of the errors could be attributed to actual cataloging deficiencies, usually failure to provide access under editor, or series, or the lack of essential cross references.

A category of errors designated as complex citation (at least to the patron) accounted for 11.4% of the requests. As noted in *The Chicago Manual of Style*, there are two basic styles of bibliographic entry, one favored by writers in literature, history and the arts which tends toward a full description and one favored by writers in the sciences where abbreviations are commonly used.[4] This latter format often results in citations which are either incomprehensible to or misinterpreted by the patron; i.e., *J. Hist. Med.* is construed as *Journal of Historical Medicine* rather than *Journal of the History of Medicine and Applied Sciences*. The study suggests that many patrons are either unfamiliar with sources for identifying abbreviations, such as CASSI (Chemical Abstracts Service Source Index) or do not take the trouble to further verify their citations. Other examples include supplements to journals cataloged as monographs, special issues of journals which patrons concluded were monographs, material republished in book form that originally appeared in journals which are owned by SUNYA and papers published in non-analyzed serials such as the Smithsonian Institution's *Annual Reports* which were assumed to be separately published monographs.

Genuine citation errors accounted for 4.6% of the requests. Some were relatively minor (i.e., Seldon for Sheldon) and were easily resolved by searching under an alternative entry (incidentally providing further confirmation that most patrons do not persevere in their search). Others, however, required extensive searching to identify the correct citation.

Requests for items in un-cataloged collections accounted for 7.7% of the total of which 4.6% were government documents, 2.7% ERIC, .2% NTIS and .2% other microform collections. It appears that imprints such as GPO, Department of Agriculture or Indiana Department of Public Instruction do not necessarily suggest to patrons that these items will be found in uncataloged collections.

Perhaps this may be due to our tendency as librarians to identify and stress the catalog as the source of information on the librarys' holdings. As Lancaster has phrased it: "A catalog is the single most important key to a library's collection. Its major function is to show whether a library owns a particular bibliographic item whose author and/or title are known (known items) and, if so, where it is located."[5] The requests in this category constituted known items since the patron knew the author and title.

The final group of errors illustrate some of the problems patrons encounter because they are unfamiliar with library terminology, procedures, policies, etc., and fail to ask for assistance or explanations.

As noted earlier, patrons at SUNYA are encouraged to search LCS as a quick substitute for the card catalog. The most commonly used search keys are the so-called author/title (actually main entry/title) and title keys. Since most bibliographical style manuals provide for entry under editor, users commonly equate editors with authorship resulting in failure. Misinterpretation of the author/title key resulted in 2.3% of the errors. The low percentage of errors in this category is probably attributable to the fact that the ILL clientele is primarily composed of faculty and graduate students who generally prefer the card catalog to the computer. Libraries planning on-line catalogs may need to overcome user resistance from an important segment of their user population.

Another 3.4% of the requests came from users who had sufficient bibliographic skills to identify the items they needed through the catalog or printout but were unable to accurately interpret the data they found. For example, the holdings statement: "[1911–45] missing issues," was interpreted to mean all issues were missing for that period rather than the Libraries' run from 1911–45 lacked some issues. Some patrons were not aware that symbols and prefixes such as *, EXT, and MIC FLM are used to designate shelving locations. One graduate student noted on her requests for journal articles that, despite repeated searches over a six month period, the volumes she needed were never in the stacks. All were on microfilm or in the current display room and were so designated on the printout.

Although the bulk of SUNYA's bound periodicals are on open shelves, a few are kept in compact storage in closed stacks. A notice is posted in the open stacks at the site where stored items would otherwise be shelved directing patrons to ask for these volumes at the Periodicals Room desk. However, several request forms inaccurately noted that SUNYA's collection of the journal began with the first volume on the open shelves.

A group of errors roughly categorized as resulting from misunderstanding of various library policies accounted for 3.9%. Several patrons assumed ILL was responsible for retrieving books from the branch library, a service provided by the Circulation Unit. Circulation (frequently staffed by student assistants) referred three patrons to ILL because specific items were missing although other usable editions were available. The largest number of requests in this category, however, are a byproduct of the Capital District Library Council's (CDLC; an area consortium) highly successful Direct Access Program which permits patrons of CDLC member institutions to borrow directly from other member institutions. A nearby college, which is frequently inundated by SUNYA students, understandably limits its participation in direct lending to faculty/staff members of other institutions. SUNYA students who study there, frequently find useful materials and ask to have them held, pending receipt of a formal ILL request. Such requests are, of course, rejected if SUNYA also owns the item.

Miscellaneous requests, including several for items missing at the time the requests were placed, accounted for the remaining 1.8% of the total.

Data was also collected relating to the users status and academic discipline. During the survey, total requests were distributed as follows: faculty 39.2%, graduate students 41.5%, undergraduates 11.5%, staff 7.6% and other 1%. Table 1 presents a cross-tabulation of type of error by status of the requester.

As can be seen from the table, different categories of users experience different problems in known item searches. So far, it appears that the adoption of AACR2 has had its primary impact on faculty and graduate students.

Cross-tabulations of type of error by academic discipline produced some interesting comparisons. By academic discipline, the largest number of requests for owned items were submitted by Anthropology (67, or 15.3%), Psychology (63, or 14.4%) and Education (32, or 7.3%). However, the number of errors as a proportion of each discipline's total requests were: Anthropology (13%), Psychology (21%) and Education (32%). The number or errors attributable to the implementation of AACR2 for these three disciplines were as follows: Anthropology (7.5%), Psychology (9.5%) and Education (15.6%).

TABLE 1
CAUSES OF USER FAILURE, BY STATUS OF SEARCHER

TYPE OF ERROR	FACULTY	GRAD	UNDERGRAD	STAFF	OTHER	ROW TOTAL
DIDN'T SEARCH	7 (10.1)	3 (1.1)	0 (.0)	0 (.0)	0 (.0)	10 (2.3)
UNSUCCESSFUL PRINTOUT SEARCH	9 (13.0)	50(18.7)	25(32.5)	4 (22.2)	2 (40.0)	90(20.6)
UNSUCCESSFUL SEARCH OF "OLD" CATALOG	5 (7.2)	28(10.4)	6 (7.8)	0 (.0)	1 (20.0)	40 (9.2)
UNSUCCESSFUL COMPUTER SEARCH	3 (4.3)	6 (2.2)	1 (1.3)	0 (.0)	0 (.0)	10 (2.3)
DIDN'T SEARCH "NEW" CATALOG	8 (11.6)	37(13.8)	1 (1.3)	2 (11.1)	0 (.0)	48 (11.0)
SERIAL NOT LISTED ON PRINTOUT	5 (7.2)	23(8.6)	4 (5.2)	0 (.0)	0 (.0)	32 (7.3)
ON ORDER	3 (4.3)	10(3.7)	0 (.0)	0 (.0)	0 (.0)	13 (3.0)
SEARCHED BY GENERIC TERM	2 (2.9)	10(3.7)	8 (10.4)	1 (5.6)	1 (20.0)	22 (5.0)
CATALOGING ERROR	5 (7.2)	11(4.1)	2 (2.6)	4 (22.2)	0 (.0)	22 (5.0)
CITATION ERROR	2 (2.9)	12(4.5)	2 (2.6)	3 (16.7)	1 (20.0)	20 (4.6)
COMPLEX CITATION	7 (10.1)	30(11.2)	11(14.3)	2 (11.1)	0 (.0)	50 (11.4)
POLICY MISUNDERSTANDING	2 (2.9)	6 (2.2)	9 (11.7)	0 (.0)	0 (.0)	17 (3.9)
CIRCULATION REFERRAL	0 (.0)	1 (.4)	2 (2.6)	0 (.0)	0 (.0)	3 (.7)
DATA MISINTERPRETATION	4 (5.8)	11(4.1)	0 (.0)	0 (.0)	0 (.0)	15 (3.4)
PERIODICAL NOT ON PRINT OUT	0 (.0)	2 (.7)	1 (1.3)	0 (.0)	0 (.0)	3 (.7)
GOVERNMENT DOCUMENTS	2 (2.9)	12 (4.5)	5 (6.5)	1 (5.6)	0 (.0)	20 (4.6)
ERIC DOCUMENTS	1 (1.4)	11(4.1)	0 (.0)	0 (.0)	0 (.0)	12 (2.7)
NATIONAL TECHNICAL INFORMATION SERVICE	0 (.0)	1 (.4)	0 (.0)	0 (.0)	0 (.0)	1 (.2)
OTHER MICROFORM	1 (1.4)	0 (.0)	0 (.0)	0 (.0)	0 (.0)	1 (.2)
MISCELLANEOUS	3 (4.3)	4 (1.5)	0 (.0)	1 (5.6)	0 (.0)	8 (1.8)
COLUMN TOTAL	69 (15.8)	268 (61.3)	77 (17.6)	18 (4.1)	5 (1.1)	437 (100.0)

This limited study suggests that the systematic collection and analysis of specific examples of user failure may provide useful data for designing library instruction programs to meet the needs of specific user groups.

This study has demonstrated that at SUNYA, the ILL office, in addition to its self-evident responsibilities, also functions as an adjunct arm of the Reference Department, providing both citation identification and one-to-one library instruction. It has also tended to confirm several of the findings of previous catalog use studies as summarized by Meyer. Specifically:

> Most people have little knowledge of the structure of the catalog. . . . People generally use authors for entry to the catalog before they use titles. . . . Most people do not persevere very long in catalog searches. More than 50% will look up only one entry and then stop, regardless of whether or not they have found what they are looking for. . . . Present catalogs are fairly adequate if the user is willing to work hard at searching.[6]

Since this study has focused on ILL as a measure of bibliographic efficiency, it has not attempted to examine other impacts of AACR2 on the ILL workload such as the conversion of the OCLC data base to AACR2. It is, at best, a preliminary investigation of AACR2 as one of many factors that contribute to use failure since it focuses only on those who persevered in their efforts. One can only speculate as to the number who did not find materials and abandoned the search without turning to either a reference librarian or ILL.

The study indicates that AACR2, as implemented at SUNYA, has contributed to user failure in known item searches resulting in an increase in ILL requests for owned items and in staff time spent explaining the structure of the catalog. However, since the study examined only catalog use failures, it precluded any assessment as to whether entries established in accordance with AACR2 contribute to greater user bibliographic efficiency than those established under previous codes.

Despite the dysfunctional aspects of the divided catalog, the overall effectiveness of the catalog was good as evidenced by the success of the ILL staff in identifying owned items. If, however, the catalog is reasonably adequate, it suggests that we, as reference librarians, must become more active in publicizing our role as specialists in the interpretation of the catalog and the use of reference tools and in encouraging patrons to ask for assistance when they do not find what they need.

REFERENCES

1. F. W. Lancaster, *The Measurement and Evaluation of Library Services* (Washington, D.C.: Information Resources Press, 1977), 19-68.
2. Franklin F. Bright, "AACR2: The First Anniversary! Celebration or Lament?" *Technicalities*, v. 2, no. 2 (June 1982): 6.
3. Alan Meyer, "Some Important Findings In Catalog Use Studies," in Lancaster, 70.
4. *The Chicago Manual of Style*. 13th ed. (Chicago: University of Chicago Press, 1982) 439-440.
5. Lancaster, 19.
6. Meyer, 69-70.

Reference Services, Serials Cataloging, and the Patron

Deborah J. Karpuk

The relationship between technical service and public service operations is unique in each library setting contingent upon communication lines and organizational design. The services, though different, share the common goal of providing service to the library patron. A study conducted by Marjorie Murfin stresses it is a misconception that placing a title in the stacks automatically assures accessibility to library patrons. Patron frustration is particularly high in retrieving serial and periodical literature held in library collections. Viewed in this way, the expertise of serial librarians in organizing library serial collections compliments and aids reference librarians in effectively assisting patrons in locating needed material. The assumption that "if they don't find it they'll ask" was not supported by the Murfin study, therefore, improving public catalog access, serials subscription lists, and the organization of serial collections is essential for increasing patron success in retrieving serial publications.[1]

ORGANIZATION

To organize serials collections is the first step in providing public service to patrons. Osborn so aptly states that serials present a unique array of problems both in the organization and cataloging of them. Titles of serials tend to change and corporate bodies or subdivisions of corporate bodies may also change.[2] Numbering and frequency fluctuations also present unique problems that serials librarians must handle in order to keep accurate records of library

---

Deborah J. Karpuk is Serials Cataloger, University of Oklahoma Libraries, Norman, Oklahoma.

© 1984 by The Haworth Press, Inc. All rights reserved.

holdings and for claiming missing issues. Osborn outlines the regularity of serials problems:

> But no one should be misled by the routine character of most publications: by no manner of means do serial irregularities occur only as rare events, only in exceptional situations. On the contrary, they are met so persistently in large research libraries that serial specialists are quite accustomed to their ways.[3]

Serials specialists are accustomed to the irregularities of serials, which are recorded in the files they maintain providing specific data on a given title. The public is rarely aware of the information available in files maintained in technical processing departments. The author is not advocating advertising technical processing files to library patrons, but that reference and public services librarians should be knowledgeable of information contained in processing files in order to refer the question or to contact the appropriate technical services area for assistance. For example, a periodical check-in card may record specific periodical issues received in the library collection and may not be available for public use. A serials record file provided for public access to the serial or periodical collection may only indicate bound volumes housed in the library collection and not show the loose issues already received.

PATRON CONFUSION

Patron confusion develops as library holdings include loose issues, bound volumes, microfiche and microfilm for the same serial or periodical title. In organizing multiple formats for the same title, it is hoped that clarity of organization is aided through separately cataloged records for each format. The patron must learn to interpret catalog cards, read location stamps, and interpret serials lists to sort out in which format and where a given title or volume is located. This process involves a basic knowledge of filing rules and rules of entry for cataloging data. Patrons who request assistance receive this instruction but the Murfin study indicates that few patrons ask.

Even the most ambitious attempt at carefully organizing and cataloging serial collections is complicated by the many times a serial publication is handled before reaching the library collection. A title is received, checked in, cataloged in full or temporarily cataloged dependent on library policy to catalog from first issue received or the first bound volume. Catalog cards are prepared, the bibliographic record may be input on-line, the volume must be stamped, marked, etc., before reaching the stacks. Each handling of the serial title increases the chance of human error. With serials, linking titles must be evaluated as well. Is the former title closed and linked to the new title or are there discrepancies in the cataloging information between the current and former title. Discrepancies in cataloging information mislead patrons and reference librarians alike. The volume and date information must be linked with appropriate titles so that reference librarians can be certain that patrons are correctly directed. Problem-solving and ironing out discrepancies create delays in the availability of the serial to the public. Consulting national databases does assist in resolving serial linking problems but can also open new avenues for evaluation as multiple interpretations of cataloging data are available on-line. On-line data may not agree with local practices which pre-date computer databases. Recataloging in each instance may not be possible. Libraries which have not closed library card catalogs may be deciding whether to split or change pre-AACR2 and AACR2 corporate headings, while building a local database with the potential as an on-line catalog. Computerized subscription lists can help reduce the number of questions directed to public service desks as well as providing information for branch locations. This information should be regularly reviewed for accuracy. If the list is not complete, patrons need to check card catalogs to be sure the library does not hold the title.

CONTROL

The statement "Someone said that controlling serials is like nailing Jello to the wall" sums up a major problem.[4] Reference librarians and non-serial specialists marvel at the serials librarian's attempts to make order from chaos and to control serials. Not only are serials costly to purchase, complicated to process and difficult to find, they are also underused, according to Barbara Pinzelik.[5] As reference librarians and public service staff provide front-line service to library patrons, a basic understanding of serials is necessary to recognize discrepancies between linking records, and misleading or inaccurate information. The library serial collection may be classified in Dewey or Library of Congress or not classified at all. Subject or corporate added entries may not indicate locations for materials in branch or special locations. These reference problems could be solved or discussed with the serials librarian or serials cataloger.

PUBLIC SERVICE

"In cases where most serials reference, including union lists and periodical directory information, is provided by the general reference department, at least one full-time member of the serials staff should be assigned in serials during prime periods to help users find volumes, explain procedures, and advise them when to return to reference for more information," states Helen Grochmal.[6] Libraries have evolved different ways in which to handle serials in both bibliographic control by serials librarians and in providing public service to library patrons. One effective approach to this problem has been to develop the integrated serials department which combines both the technical services aspects of serials along with public service aspects of serials. This arrangement is no substitute for in-depth reference service but when serials services are divided up, contact is lost between the initial receipt of the title and the ultimate purpose for acquiring the material. One recent study stresses the strength given to providing effective public service through this departmental arrangement. The integrated serials departmental arrangement allows active interaction between public service serials staff and those involved in serials technical service operations having direct access to serials processing files which may provide additional information needed by patrons. Through this arrangement, a serials expertise is developed with service as the ultimate goal.[7]

REFERENCE SERVICE

Linking bibliographic information with service operations is essential in providing quality public service, whatever organizational arrangement exists between serials technical services and public service operations in the library. Nancy Jean Melin stresses "A truly integrated flow of serials from order and receipt to cataloging and finally to reference work should be thought of as the ideal."⁸ She continues "Successful reference work with periodicals depends upon an intimate acquaintance with the abstracts and indexes that access their contents."⁹ In organizing serials collections it is helpful to understand how the serial title is indexed, and how citations appear from which patrons access a title, specific volume or issue number. If indexed differently than from the way the library has cataloged the material, users may find difficulty in locating the material and give up their search. Consulting with reference librarians prior to cataloging difficult serial titles can help in providing the required bibliographic access necessary for locating the material. This helps the serials cataloger understand how patrons will reach the information from sources other than the public card catalog, serials lists, etc.

Science serials are particularly problematic. A recent example involved an AIChE Symposium Series title *Heat transfer*. *Heat transfer* had been cataloged under the corporate entry American Institute of Chemical Engineers with *Heat transfer* as the title. During the course of its publication since 1953, the series entry had changed from Chemical Engineering Progress Symposium Series with a series volume numbering to AIChE Symposium Series with a series volume numbering. To complicate matters, *Heat transfer* had its own volume numbering plus date and the National Heat Transfer Conference, an added entry and from which *Heat transfer* emanates, had conference numbering for the conference proceedings. Not all conference proceedings comprise *Heat transfer*. This serials cataloging problem surfaced through the engineering reference librarian and an able staff member at the Engineering Library. No series added entry had been provided for *Heat transfer*, yet it was through the Chemical Engineering Progress Symposium Series and the appropriate series volume number and the later series title, AIChE Symposium Series and its volume number that patrons reach *Heat transfer* through the engineering indexes. Both series include many other titles. Serials cataloging policy did not include providing series added entries for serials. An exception to this policy was made in order to aid patrons by providing series access in the public catalog.

Similar assistance had been provided by other reference librarians spanning difficult materials in all subject areas. In particular, it was useful to learn that though most geological fieldtrip guidebooks have distinctive titles, the geological indexes refer only to the appropriate geological survey, and fieldtrip guidebook number. Analytics of the geological guidebooks were not requested due to this fact. With the quantity of guidebooks published, this was a relief to the serials cataloger. These examples show how reference librarians and technical services librarians can work in tandem to solve common problems and to evaluate or set library policy which would affect both areas.

PROBLEM SOLVING

In handling problems which span rule changes and multiple complications, consulting with reference librarians and recruiting their assistance in problem-solving is mutually beneficial. From an organizational standpoint in which public access to serial publications is provided through organizing the serials collection and providing bibliographic access to the collection, additional information as discussed above aids the cataloger in doing a better job. Reference librarians also become aware of problems routinely faced by serials catalogers, developing further understanding of serial irregularities and problems. Both the serials cataloger and reference librarian benefit from the exchange and, ultimately, the patron becomes the recipient of better service.

Unless the card catalog has been completely converted to machine-readable format and into an on-line catalog, library patrons and librarians alike are still reliant on the card catalog. Access points are limited and catalog maintenance expensive. Backlogs of cards requiring correction plague cataloging staff. The card file requires precise or nearly, precise knowledge, to find the required title. Manual card catalogs do not have the flexibility of computer databases for searching and finding citations with less than precise information. Current serials subscription lists may not include all library serial holdings, unless a complete serial catalog conversion has taken place. Patrons and public service librarians must not confuse the convenience of the paper list with the more complete card catalog. Lists should be reviewed regularly for accuracy and errors spotted should be reported. The correction process is multi-faceted and slow depending on the complexity of the problem; problem-solving requires cooperation, communication and patience. Reference librarians and technical services librarians must acknowledge the strengths and limitations of the current technology. As on-line catalogs are a goal of college and academic libraries, cataloging problems will need to be solved before conversion will be complete.

Perpetuating errors will continue to mislead patrons; perpetuating serials cataloging errors may make the material inaccessible. Reference librarians, serials librarians and the patron have a stake in building a better, flexible and accurate serials file.

CONCLUSION

To organize serial collections is the essential beginning for providing public service. The serial literature of today provides the most current research available in many fields. The proliferation of serial titles is claiming a bigger slice of the acquisitions budget, yet studies have shown that patron frustration is high when specific entries are not available in the card catalog, or when the information is complicated and confusing. A low percentage of library patrons request bibliographic assistance. Serial publications may span several formats and several branch library locations. The indexes and abstracts used for retrieving serial citations may also be located in several areas in the library. User frustration increases with more referrals from one point to another. It is essential that reference librarians and public services staff develop a greater understanding of the problems in organizing serial publications. Conversely, serials catalogers and serials librarians must understand how serial publications are indexed and used by library patrons so as to provide the access or additional access necessary for facilitating the easy location of serial titles. Serials automation systems are still in the developmental stage. Few libraries have the luxury of a fully automated system or a complete on-line catalog and must rely on a mix of on-line files, card catalogs and periodical subscription lists. Cataloging serials involves a blending of pre-computer, pre-AACR2, AACR2 and information available on-line with currently existing policies and catalogs in the library. In cooperation, both serials librarians and reference librarians can better achieve their common goal—providing the best service possible to the library patron.

REFERENCES

1. Marjorie E. Murfin, "The Myth of Accessibility: Frustration & Failure in Retrieving Periodicals," *The Journal of Academic Librarianship*, 6:16-19 (Mar. 1980).
2. Andrew D. Osborn, *Serial Publications: Their Place and Treatment in Libraries.* 3d ed. (Chicago: American Library Association, 1980), p. 223.

3. Osborn, *Serial Publications*, p. 241.

4. Anne Marie Allison, "Automated Serials Control: A Bibliographic Survey," in *Management of Serials Automation: Current Technology & Strategies for Future Planning*, edited by Peter Gellatly, (New York: Haworth Press, 1982), p. 5.

5. Barbara P. Pinzelik, "The Serials Maze: Providing Public Service for a Large Serials Collection," *The Journal of Academic Librarianship*, 8:89-94 (May 1982).

6. Helen M. Grochmal, "The Serials Department's Responsibilities for Reference," *RQ*, 20:403-406 (Summer 1981).

7. Sue Anne Harrington and Deborah J. Karpuk, "The Integrated Serials Department: Its Value Today and in the Future," unpublished manuscript.

8. Nancy Jean Melin, "The Public Service Functions of Serials," *Serials Review*, 6:39-44 (Jan./Mar. 1980).

9. Melin, "The Public Service Functions of Serials," p. 43.

SUBJECT ORGANIZATION AND ACCESS

The Flaw of Subject Access in the Library Catalog: An Opinion

Norman D. Stevens

In a recent editorial in *Information Technology and Libraries* Pauline A. Cochrane points out that studies of the use of existing online public access catalogs show that "the great majority of users are performing *topical subject* searches."[1] This, she points out, confirms the findings of some earlier catalog use studies and argues for the need for greater attention to subject analysis and subject access in the online public access catalog. Ms. Cochrane is not alone in this effort. Phyllis Richmond, another leading catalog theorist, also discusses "Futuristic Aspects of Subject Access"[2] in a recent issue of *Library Resources & Technical Services*. Taken by the apparent degree to which users turn to the online public access catalog for subject information, and the evident ease with which new and nifty ways of providing subject, or at least pseudo-subject, analysis, there is a rush by designers of these new catalogs and library planners to assume responsibility for providing subject analysis and subject access to information as a key component of these new tools. A recent report by the Council on Library Resources on *Subject Access* states as an assumption that "the optimum subject search tool is the online public access catalog equipped with sophisticated search capabilities including natural language and controlled vocabulary searches."[3]

Norman D. Stevens is Librarian, University of Connecticut, Storrs, CT 06269.

© 1984 by The Haworth Press, Inc. All rights reserved.

Certainly improvement is needed. Exhortations and efforts such as those mentioned, including those of CLR, are welcome. The flaws of the past in terms of the extent and nature of subject access in the card catalog are clearly evident. There are too few entry points for the material in the catalog; the quality of subject analysis has often been extremely poor; and the use of outmoded terminology, which it is difficult, for both practical and psychological reasons, to update is a severe limitation. There has been no shortage of articles and books demonstrating those shortcomings of the card catalog as a tool for subject access. Efforts to correct those flaws and to substantially improve the level and quality of subject access in the library catalog are much needed, long overdue, and clearly welcome.

Unfortunately we tend to look for simple solutions and we tend to ignore the past. Few of the online public access catalog designers are likely to take the time and the effort—although they should—to read Francis Miksa's new book *The Subject in the Dictionary Catalog from Cutter to the Present.* It is especially disappointing to note that the CLR conference, did not include historians like Miksa. That is disappointing because the quality of Miksa's writing and the logic of his thinking, especially in his chapter of "Summary and Observations," have far more to say to us on this subject than the simplistic thoughts of the CLR report. In particular Miksa's opinion that "the role of user considerations, at least in the way they are presently conceived and applied, must be allowed to die an honorable death"[4] is significant. Likewise we need to heed his caution that "the time has come to take seriously the professional nature of subject information systems engineering."[5]

In our rush to judgment on this issue, whether we take Miksa's ideas into account or not, we also need to think about the underlying major flaw in the provision of subject access which has been characteristic of the card catalog and will, at least in the foreseeable future, certainly continue to be true of the online public access catalog. In seeking to overcome the apparent flaws of subject access we must not lose sight of this major flaw either in the design of those catalogs or in our efforts to persuade patrons to use the catalog for subject information. We need to continue to caution them about its major limitations. Libraries have for a long time abdicated responsibility for direct access to a broad range of subject information. What we have provided in our catalogs is, at best, a limited approach to the subject content of a small part of our collections. We have concentrated our efforts, in terms of the provision of local bibliographic records, on the identification and description of discrete physical units, whether those be books, periodicals, maps, or other items. We have created in the catalog a tool which does a reasonably complete job of providing information about all of those units within the library. The user, and the librarian, can approach the catalog with a known-item search in hand with reasonable confidence that, if he/she knows how to use the catalog, a successful search can be completed that will indicate whether or not the library owns the particular item. Whether or not it is actually on the shelf is, of course, something else.

To use the catalog for subject information is quite another situation. At its very best, even in the more sophisticated forms that an online catalog can provide, the catalog can provide only very partial and incomplete information about the availability of information on a particular subject in that library's collections. A topical subject search for a few books that might touch on a subject is one thing. Seeking specific subject information is another. The wealth of subject information contained in any library's collection, even a small library, not just in the discrete physical units contained in the catalog but in the discrete bibliographic units more adequately dealt with in a range of indexing and abstracting services, subject bibliographies, and other tools is something else again. We need to be careful not to mislead the user into thinking that he/she will find the same degree and level of information in the catalog when conducting a subject search as will be true with a known-item search. Any effort to improve subject access to information through the catalog which assumes that the catalog, at least as it now exists, can be a major means for identifying and locating information on a subject basis is sadly mistaken. We need to begin to identify ways in which the vastly superior subject access to information found in indexing and abstracting services and similar tools can be effectively integrated with the online catalog. Given our past neglect we should not expect the online catalog to be the sole source for subject information. For at least the foreseeable future the competent reference librarian will be, in my opinion, a far better guide to the location of information on a subject in the library's collection than any online catalog yet available or planned. We must not fail to recognize that. We should not expect to substitute efforts at subject analysis on the part of catalogers for those broader professional skills. If patrons want good subject information, and if we expect to provide them with that information, the online public access catalog, with whatever subject access it may provide, will have to be complemented with reference librarians.

NOTES

1. Pauline A. Cochrane "A Paradigm Shift in Library Science," *Information Technology and Libraries* 2:3- 4, 1983.
2. Phyllis A. Richmond "Futuristic Aspects of Subject Access," *Library Resources & Technical Services* 27:88-93, 1983.
3. *Subject Access.* Washington, D.C., Council on Library Resources, 1982. p. 68.
4. Francis Miksa *The Subject in the Dictionary Catalog from Cutter to the Present.* Chicago, ALA, 1983. p. 404.
5. *Ibid.*, p. 410.

User Categories and User Convenience in Subject Cataloging

Francis Miksa

INTRODUCTION[1]

One of the most pervasive beliefs of American subject catalogers is that the subject heading element of the dictionary catalog should be constructed on the principle of user convenience. In its narrowest sense, this means that individual subject headings should be chosen on the basis of what terms are commonly used by patrons in their subject searching. Charles A. Cutter had this in mind in his discussion of equally useful compound subject names: "When there is any decided usage (*i.e.* custom of the public to designate the subjects by one of the names rather than by the others) let it be followed.[2] In a broader sense the idea of user convenience means that *all* aspects of subject heading work—choices concerning specificity, term syntax, synonyms, etc.—should reflect the way users approach the catalog. David J. Haykin, the first chief of the Subject Cataloging Division of the Library of Congress, expressed this more comprehensive view in 1951 when he concluded that, "the reader is the focus in all cataloging principles and practice."[3]

The chief difficulty with these conceptions, and one which has led some to doubt the idea of user convenience, is their vagueness in referring to users. It is not enough to say that the subject heading system should be convenient to users. One must also be able to identify in some meaningful way who the users are that are to be served and what constitutes their "convenience." Paul S. Dunkin, among others, questioned whether this could be done:

> Is there such a creature as "the user"; or are there (as with costs) many users each with his individual habits?. . . Even if

---

Francis Miksa is Acting Dean, School of Library and Information Science, Louisiana State University, Baton Rouge, Louisiana.

we find "the user," can we safely build our practice to fit him—or shall we keep on making studies to find out if "the user" (just as you and I) changes habits and ways of thinking from time to time?[4]

Dunkin's questions to the contrary, subject catalogers have not been remiss in identifying users and what is necessary for making the subject catalog convenient for them. They have done so in terms of user categories—identifying users in terms of recognizable groups. The makeup of these user categories has changed significantly over the years, however, and aspects of user categories, especially those more recently identified, raise questions as to whether they are a meaningful way to conceptualize patrons at all.

The purpose of this paper is to summarize and offer critical observations about the kinds of user categories to which subject catalogers have resorted over the years. It is assumed that the usefulness of this task is not limited to what it says for subject catalogers alone, but extends as well to other kinds of library professionals—in the case here to reference librarians—insofar as they too tend to justify their work on the basis of user categories and their characteristics.[5]

CUTTER AND USER CONVENIENCE[6]

Charles A. Cutter, who is generally thought of as the father of the dictionary catalog and the first to state the idea of user convenience, divided the library's public into three general kinds of "inquirers":

1. those who want something quickly;
2. those who want to make a thorough study of some specific subject; and
3. those who want to study fully some general class of subjects.[7]

He concluded that the first group was the "loudest and largest" of the three. While this group was most dependent on a catalog and was, in fact, the reason for the popularity of the "ordinary dictionary catalogue," its members were essentially "desultory" in their approach to books, subject searching, and the use of the library in general. They were impatient, wanting an answer for their book search as quickly as possible, regardless of what that yielded. They were also generally undisciplined in their searching and, in fact, "averse to mental effort," often uncomprehending of the fact that useful information might be found under synonymous terms or that topics were by definition part of a structured universe of subjects. What they most often searched for were books that were listed under captions for general categories of literature—as if to say, "I want a philosophical work" or "I want a fiction work" or "I want a religious work." In Cutter's opinion, they did not care "about the particular subject of the book so much as whether it be well written and interesting."[8]

The other two groups of inquirers were set apart from the first by two essential factors. First, to varying degrees they approached subject searching with an awareness of classificatory subject relationships. Second, to varying degrees they understood that subject searching was tantamount to disciplined investigation that required patience, effort, and the realization that not all their needs could be met by any catalog. These two categories differed essentially only in the breadth of their searching strategy. The second group tended to focus on specific subjects, aware of the need, for example, to find the various works on those subjects and compare them critically as to their worth, but not always insistent on searching for such topics in terms of their larger classificatory relationships. In contrast, the third group tended to approach any subject search in terms of a strong sense of classificatory structure, beginning broadly and working downward to the more specific elements of the whole.

Some of the foregoing characteristics of Cutter's user categories might well be familiar to the modern cataloger or reference librarian. For example, in the course of meeting the public, what librarian has not encountered at least occasionally the aimless user whose appreciation of the library's attempts to organize its resources for subject access are almost nil; or in contrast, the patron who approaches a subject area in such a structured way that any variation from that structure appears as a hindrance.

What will not be generally apparent among moderns, however, is the fact that Cutter's user categories and characteristics actually arose from a highly structured and uniform sense of the universe of subjects and from a well-developed psychology of the public. Both of these factors came from his exposure to the tenets of the philosophical school called Scottish common sense realism commonly taught at most American institutions of higher education before the Civil War. Cutter did not approach the universe of subjects represented in the subject heading system as a conglomerate of separate specialized fields each with their own unique logics and structures, but rather as a unified whole. Furthermore, he subdivided that unitary universe of knowledge into classes and subclasses not only by intrinsic logical relationships within cohesive subject areas, but even more so by a categorical approach to subjects themselves. In his system, specificity or the degree of narrowness in any particular subject was a function of the relative degree of concreteness or abstraction that the subject term represented. Thus, great specificity meant greater concreteness whereas great breadth referred to greater abstractness. On this basis, the subject relationships between all subjects could be determined with some facility. And because they could be so determined, both the subject catalogers and the user (once having learned the idea of degrees of concreteness) could predict entry patterns and citation order in the system with consistency and ease.

User categories were also not distinct and mutually exclusive for Cutter, but actually elements of a single continuum of use. Desultory and advanced readers were differentiated not in some absolute way but rather only in terms of the respective development of the same set of mental powers that all readers had. In short, there was no essential difference between the basic mental structure and thinking processes of any of the three categories of inquirers. Their minds functioned in the same way. The only difference was in the way the minds of the different categories of users had been educated (i.e., cultivated) and, therefore, how much of their natural mental potential for knowledge acquisition was brought to the subject searching process. Desultory readers, because of their lack of mental conditioning, tended to search only for the simplest of subjects—those that were most concrete (i.e., works about individual subjects represented especially as persons or places)—whereas advanced readers went well beyond such simple or specific subjects either by searching under equivalent meanings or by searching subjects of greater generality (i.e., of less concreteness). In either case advanced readers developed search strategies that depended on their varying knowledge of the unitary universe of knowledge of which all subjects occupied categorical positions. The essential point to be noted was that any desultory reader could through mental exercise and self improvement move into the other categories in a natural way. The groups were not in effect separated by some insurmountable and necessary barrier.

Cutter's sense of unity in the world of subjects and among users had a striking effect on his approach to the subject element of the dictionary catalog. The most important result was that it allowed Cutter to justify the specific entry structure of his dictionary subject catalog. Specific entry, which required entry of a work under the single most concrete subject treated in the work—especially persons and places—was necessary because the largest class of users (desultory readers) would be most helped by that approach. At the same time, advanced readers were also served by his catalog because the various specific entries had been tied together with an infrastructure of cross-references that referred from subjects of greater generality to concrete and, therefore, more specific subjects and by subarranging the works under specific entries by terms of greater generality that would indicate to advanced readers the broader topics to which the specific or concrete topics were related.

Cutter's sense of unity also allowed him to justify particular subject heading decisions related to user convenience. For example, in the common absence of any indications of which one of several equivalent compound subject names in a book was to be chosen as the heading he regularly chose the one that began with terms of greater rather than lesser concreteness because it was more likely to be looked up by the largest class of inquirers. At the same time, advanced inquirers, those of the second and third types, would be provided with great predictability in subject searching. Given a subject search of any coordinated set of subjects, one need only look under the more concrete subject in the coordination to see if it were in the catalog. If it were not found, one might then look under the less concrete topic to see if there were some more general works that upon close examination included the more concrete qualification in their texts. It was this kind of predictability that was the basis of Cutter's remarks that his specific entry system provided "facility of reference."[9] He meant that because the system always had a most specific or concrete beginning point for entry, all categories of inquirers could depend upon it in a predictable way.

USER CATEGORIES: SHIFTING IDEAS AT THE TURN OF THE CENTURY[10]

Cutter introduced the foregoing ideas about users and subject headings during the mid-1870s and did not thereafter alter them in any significant way. In fact, there is a distinct sense that when he wrote them they were already outdated because the Scottish thinking upon which they were based was already a century old and fast being replaced by such newer currents of thought as idealism and pragmatism. Thus, when the fourth and posthumous edition of his *Rules* were published in 1904, it is not surprising that a new generation of subject catalogers, while just as concerned about user convenience as Cutter had been, was expressing that concern in a way significantly different than Cutter had expressed it in the subject heading section of his *Rules*.

Several different aspects of this newer point of view are important to note. First, the unitary universe of subjects and subject relationships that had been fundamental to Cutter's approach to subject access was already beginning to disintegrate into the more familiar twentieth century panoply of subjects as a vast array of widely divergent fields each of which has a distinct and unique classification structure. No better example of this change can be found than in the construction of the Library of Congress Classification between 1898 and 1910, where the scheme was developed as a series of relatively separate topical areas united superficially only by a vague overall organizational structure and by such mechanical internal arrangement features as alphabetical, chronological and geographical subdivision patterns. Second, the notion of scholarly endeavor itself was changing at an accelerated pace. In Cutter's scheme of things a scholar referred to a person whose mental cultivation was sufficiently advanced that he or she pursued subject knowledge with an understanding of the uniform classificatory structure of the singular universe of subjects and their relationships. By the first decade of the twentieth century, however, a scholar was already coming to mean one who had become familiar with or who was in the process of learning a special segment of the universe of subjects. In other words, a scholar (and the idea of scholarliness) was becoming defined not simply by *how* a person knew what he knew, but more importantly by *what* he knew in terms of a specialized subject area.[11] Third, the organization of professional library interests had become sufficiently advanced that the library movement itself began to be self-differentiated into the more specialized library interests and tasks. This, in turn, provided a basis for two essentially new approaches to user categories that, when combined with the idea of special areas of knowledge and the notion of specialist scholars, had a profound effect on how user categories and, therefore, user convenience were viewed. Those approaches were library differentiation by size and library differentiation by type.

LIBRARY DIFFERENTIATION BY SIZE[12]

The first decisive break in the cohesiveness of the expanding American professional library community after its beginnings in 1876 occurred as librarians began to differentiate their tasks and needs in terms of the relative sizes of their libraries. Specifically, librarians from small, often rural or small town libraries and midwestern in location, found themselves at odds with librarians from larger, principally urban, public libraries, often located in the East. The conflict between these segments of the professional library community was expressed in such ways as the rise of competing organizations both within and outside the ALA, the growth and role of the ALA Council, the concern of the ALA Publishing Board especially between 1895 and 1915 to publish practical works for librarians of small libraries and, ultimately, the move of ALA headquarters in 1909 to the Midwest.[13]

Subject catalogers expressed this same conflict in a period of public debate during the first decade of the twentieth century by focusing their attention on the differences between subject catalogs made for large libraries and those made for small libraries. It should be noted that the fact that such a debate took place at all was due to the advent of readily available subject heading copy, first after 1895 in the form of the *ALA List of Subject Headings*, and, second, after 1901 in the form of subject headings included on the printed cards of the Library of Congress. Prior to those innovations, subject catalogers either had to devise their own subject headings or copy the subject headings found in exemplary printed catalogs. Because both methods were difficult, however, they tended to discourage subject catalog construction. In contrast, the appearance of readily available subject heading copy brought the reality of subject catalogs within the reach of every library.

The use of lists and copy for card catalogs brought about two unique difficulties of their own. First, their availability began the long tradition of list-oriented subject cataloging in which the idea of making subject headings that adequately expressed subject specialization in particular instances became subservient to subject heading choices more or less confined to those headings already devised by the authorities who supplied the headings. Second, and more important for the discussion here, subject heading lists, with their extensive subheadings, and subject heading copy found on catalog cards promoted a new sense of what a subject heading was. Prior to this time a subject heading was considered the lead term above a columnar listing of works in a printed dictionary catalog (i.e., it was a subject term at the "head" of each such list or file). Any particular listing might also be subarranged by still other terms placed among the entries below the heading but those terms were not technically a part of the heading. Their separation from the heading was emphasized by the use of different type faces for each. In contrast, card catalogs required that a heading and its subarrangement terms be listed together as a string-of-terms on the top of a unit card entry. This format change encouraged subject catalogers to identify the entire string-of-terms found together on the top of any one card as a subject heading rather than only the conventionally named initial term found in the string. And identification of entire strings-of-terms as subject headings in turn raised questions of complexity in syntax that had not previously been encountered. In fact, questions of complexity constituted the chief issue that highlighted the public discussion of the differences between subject catalogs made respectively for large or for small libraries.

Small libraries was the common term used to identify a cohesive group of institutions that included smaller and medium-sized public libraries, and branches of large urban libraries, and libraries or departments of libraries that served children. Large libraries included the main headquarters of urban libraries and academic libraries of all kinds. A moment's reflection will show that the difference between these groups was not actually the physical size of the libraries involved nor even in many respects the sizes of their collections, although collection size was important. Rather, the chief difference was in the kinds of clientele they served. It was concluded that large libraries principally served what had come to be known by the turn of the century as scholars and students, those patrons who used books and searched for subjects in a serious and disciplined manner. These users had the skills necessary for using such subject access tools as complex dictionary subject catalogs, subject bibliographies, and classified catalogs; in short, bibliographical tools that were generally sophisticated in their structure and that arranged subjects with some regard to their classificatory relationships. In contrast, small libraries primarily served that much more extensive population of readers whose bibliographical skills and intellectual motivation were thought to be much less developed and, in many cases almost non-existent. The former were characterized as above-average, the latter as average readers.

The similarity between these two categories of users and Cutter's categories of users is striking. Cutter had also envisioned a range of users that at either extreme appeared to include the same characteristics as those listed here. But this is as far as the similarity goes. The user groups representing extremes in Cutter's portrayal of the public, while differing in their abilities in somewhat the same way, retained an important likeness. They all functioned with the same mental processes, their differences owing only to the lack of the development of mental potential among average or desultory readers. Here, the two groups were essentially different. The notion of advanced or above-average readers which implied the kind of subject specialization already described as having occurred by the turn of the century suggested that scholars and students were different from average readers not simply because of their intellectual skills, but also because of their specialist training. In practical terms this meant that the two kinds of users were different in kind as well as in degree and that there was a necessary and significant gap between them. Furthermore where Cutter's approach to users led him to conclude that the same subject system might structurally serve the entire range of users, here for the first time one finds the conclusion that libraries of either type and, therefore, library users were different to such a degree that the subject catalogs that served each group must also be different in some significant way. Incorporating that difference in subject heading systems constructed for the two kinds of libraries—large and small—was the essential question addressed during the first decade public debate on subject cataloging.

Subject catalogs made for large libraries with their primarily more sophisticated and specialist scholar and student users required headings of greater specificity. This meant that headings were needed that more nearly matched the topical scopes of the increasingly "minute" (i.e., more specific) subjects of a growing volume of publications then beginning to be issued by an active and expanding scholarly press. These catalogs also required the use of greater numbers of subdivision devices in order to control the length of individual subject heading files. And, most importantly, because subject heading workers remained committed to the idea that headings must represent a serious attempt to use conventional subject names, they had to resort to still other devices that controlled the normal scattering that the use of conventional subject names promoted.

The most important effort to fulfill these needs occurred in the initial development of the subject heading system of the Library of

Congress between 1898 and 1910. J. C. M. Hanson, the chief architect of the system, was aware from the beginning that the Library of Congress system needed large numbers of complex headings to meet its needs. He also incorporated significant incursions of classificatory sequencing in the architecture of the system, some of it by the outright choice of undivided class entry terms, some of it by the outright choice of divided class entry strings-of-terms, and much of it by the use of manipulated heading syntax, especially through inversion. As a result, the Library of Congress subject heading system that Hanson created was not a pure dictionary subject catalog of the kind that Cutter had designed but rather a hybrid catalog of a distinctly unique cast. Its classificatory features were especially striking because the various classificatory sequences chosen for inclusion in the subject catalog reflected and were often based on the Library's classification scheme then being developed. In other words, choosing one or another subject area collocation pattern in the subject heading system functioned as a shadow of the classification scheme, sometimes following it closely, sometimes purposefully providing its opposite, but in each case bound to the same kind of field-by-field special subject structure that characterized the shelf scheme. Hanson's justification for the results of these measures was not to deny their classificatory basis (in this case, a strong bent towards alphabetico-classed structure), but rather to claim its necessity in light of the fact that the Library of Congress' chief clientele then and presumably in the future consisted of scholars and students who needed that kind of subject catalog structure.

In contrast to the foregoing, advocates of subject catalogs for small libraries loudly called for subject catalog simplication that would more readily serve the needs of average readers. They faced a formidable task, however, On the one hand, the chief source of such headings, the ALA *List*, the second 1898 edition of which had been reprinted several times, had no ongoing organization like the Library of Congress to keep it current. The task was also formidable because the basis for simplicity that matched the needs of users was not known.

Some direction toward solving the latter problem was suggested by Theresa Hitchler who noted in her 1905 *Cataloging for Small Libraries* that choices in subject heading terminology for average users in small libraries should be based on observations of what such users ask for and how their minds work.[14] When, thereafter, in the attempt to solve the problem of an updated list to be compiled, the first editor of the new edition, Esther Crawford took up Hitchler's challenge of identifying just what that terminology should be. Through a series of articles in the *Library Journal*, Crawford requested catalogers of small libraries to send their observations to her about appropriate choices for a great number of individual subject terms.[15] Unfortunately, her findings were inconclusive and she was able to make few such determinations with any finality.

A new edition of the list was eventually completed by Mary Josephine Briggs, Crawford's successor on the project. But Briggs' resolutions of the problem of terminology and syntax choices had a significant effect on how the notion of user convenience was to develop in the succeeding decades. First, Briggs concluded that consistency in subject heading terminology was neither obtainable nor necessary because average users themselves were fundamentally unpredictable in the way they used subject terminology. Second, where evidence gathered by Crawford indicated any particular patterns or choices, she followed it. As a practical solution for the much larger number of instances in which no evidence was forthcoming, however, she simply followed Library of Congress choices and patterns. This not only had the effect of incorporating into the ALA *List* much of the classificatory structure of the Library of Congress subject heading system but labeling the result as acceptable for small libraries and their average users. Third, she suggested in almost an offhanded way what eventually would become a significantly new approach to categorizing users—that is, that grouping users by type of library was a more adequate way to deal with how subject catalog choices should be made.[16]

LIBRARY DIFFERENTIATION BY TYPE[17]

The differentiation of libraries by the types they represent, like differentiation by size, also began late in the last century. But its basic nomenclature—academic libraries, public libraries, school libraries, and special libraries—did not become fully standardized until after the First World War. This typology is important in the development of subject cataloging in two ways. First, at about the same time that the above nomenclature became widely accepted, subject cataloging (along with the entire field of librarianship) entered an era of significant self examination and reflection that ultimately led to the identification of library science as an explicit field of study. Accompanying that intellectual shift in perspective was a significant number of works that, in the course of attempting to explain various elements of the field in a more rigorous fashion than previous writings, adopted the new nomenclature. This was no less exemplified than in subject cataloging, for example, in both the first edition in 1930 of Margaret Mann's classic work, *Introduction to Cataloging and the Classification of Books* and the 1933 explanation of subject heading work provided by Minnie Earl Sears in the third edition of her *List of Subject Headings for Small Libraries*. These works were striking in their attempts to provide some kind of rational explanation of the subject cataloging process in the context of types of libraries. They were especially important because little of importance had been written on the topic since the first decade of the century, a period during which subject cataloging had had to face such new problems as the increasing size of catalogs and the first calls by library administrators for catalogers to assume greater responsibility for cataloging costs. Their subsequent adoption in the field as basic works helped to ensure that the categorization of users by type of library and the application of those categories to subject cataloging were also adopted.

The second reason why the appearance of a new type of library nomenclature was important in the development of subject cataloging was that, following Briggs' comments in the third edition of the ALA *List*, it provided a more convenient, seemingly more logical, and obviously more refined approach to users and their convenience in subject heading work than categorizations by size had provided. In this approach, the clientele of a particular type of library was viewed as having unique characteristics that set it apart from the clienteles of other types of libraries. Thus, if one could identify the most salient features of the subject searching characteristics of the users of a particular type of library, it then seemed reasonable to assume that subject headings could be tailored to the needs of that kind of user. For example, following this reasoning, it seemed logical to assume that because the children who searched for subjects in children's or school libraries approached their task with relatively simplistic ideas, the subject headings in children's libraries must necessarily be "simple" rather than complex. Likewise, because patrons of special libraries more often than not used specialized terminology in their subject searching, that same specialized terminology must necessarily be incorporated into the subject heading vocabulary of the catalogs used by them. Only in this way could subject catalogs for either type of library clientele be made user convenient.

THE FAILURE OF USER CATEGORIES BASED ON TYPES OF LIBRARIES[18]

The concept that user convenience was oriented to the user categories associated with types of libraries flourished for approximately three decades to the 1950s and in some respects still continues, particularly in efforts to provide special subject heading lists or thesauri for particular kinds of special libraries and collections. Ultimately it too, like user categorization by size of library, failed to provide an adequate basis for determining user convenience in subject heading work. There are three probable reasons for that failure. First, although categorizing users by type of library seemed like a logical way to speak of highly distinctive types of libraries such as special libraries associated with well-defined special fields of inquiry, the logic behind it broke down for other types of libraries that were not associated with special subject fields. Thus, Margaret Mann in 1930 and, following her, Julia Pettee in 1946, after having put forward elaborate schemes of types of libraries, found little that could distinguish, say, public libraries from academic libraries except general differences between scholarly users and average users of the kind that had been current decades earlier. With that limited basis upon which to devise specific procedures, Mann for one could do little more than suggest that subject headings in public library catalogs be kept relatively simple in formulation and length. She suggested this both as an aid to generally unsophisticated public library users and as a way to keep file length under individual headings from becoming too small. Likewise, a close examination of Elva S. Smith's arguments in favor of simple headings for children's and school libraries will show that the notion of simple headings; based as it was on the analogy of simplicity in the subject searching habits of children, was actually a very indistinct concept.[19]

The second reason why differentiation of users by type of library failed to provide an adequate basis for making subject catalogs user convenient was that after more than two decades of user studies, themselves based for the most part on types of libraries, no extensive objective evidence was ever uncovered to support the basic equation that users can be adequately characterized by the types of libraries they frequent. If anything was concluded by the mid-1950s, in fact (besides, that is, the frustration of inconclusiveness), it was a reformulation of user categorization similar to that found at the beginning of the century. Studies appeared to show that there were actually only two essentially distinct kinds of users—specialists and general users—and that these appear in all kinds of libraries in varying proportions.

There were differences between the reformulation of the 1950s and the user categories proposed in the earlier period, of course. For one thing, the two categories of users were no longer tied to library size. For another, the subject heading system in the dictionary catalog had by the 1950s become indelibly associated with general users, this despite arguments proposed by Julia Pettee that suggested how a dictionary subject catalog made for general users should and could be made to differ from that constructed for scholars and specialists. This association of the dictionary subject catalog primarily with general users was aided in no small part by the identification of adequate subject access tools for specialized libraries with the spate of new methods that appeared after the late 1940s. The most notable advances of the latter kind were faceted classification schemes and coordinate indexing systems. The identification of the dictionary subject catalog with general users was also aided by an even deeper chasm that had appeared between general and specialist users in attempts to characterize them. Some indication of this increasingly radical separation may be found in Pettee's analysis in 1946. There, Pettee described the academic scholar with attributes very much like those found in descriptions of specialists who used special libraries. Further, she pictured the academic scholar as existing in an almost rarefied intellectual atmosphere while searching for subject information. This in turn contrasted sharply with Pettee's description of the general user as for the most part intellectually inept and frivolous, needful mainly of "casual" information. Finally, Pettee's subsequent characterization of the dictionary subject catalog made for scholars and specialists as little more than a starting point for research which was actually of little help in finding very discrete bits of information that scholars and specialists needed, and her characterization of the dictionary subject catalog made for general users as a kaleidoscope of temporary encyclopedic references, replete with a great deal of redundant entry, and ever changing to meet new popular subject demands, provided little assurance that the dictionary catalog subject heading system could ever be much more than a very imprecise subject access tool. In short, the dictionary subject catalog was useful mainly for the imprecise subject searching needs of general users.[20]

The third reason why differentiation of users by type of library failed to provide an adequate basis for making the dictionary subject catalog user convenient resided in the increasing importance and dominance of subject heading lists and copy, especially that which was supplied by the Library of Congress. This ensured that problems associated with Library of Congress headings and with its questionable approach to user convenience became the problems of all libraries that depended on its subject cataloging products.[21]

By 1940 Library of Congress subject headings had become much more complex than J. C. M. Hanson had, perhaps, ever imagined possible. Subject heading syntax variation and inconsistency had increased to a noticeable degree so that a variety of syntax patterns—brief headings, extended but straightforward phrase headings, inverted and other forms of phrase headings, and strings-of-term headings involving subdivisions—all competed as legitimate subject heading forms. Furthermore, the way headings were used to specify the subjects of books had also come to vary greatly, particularly as the use of multiple entry terms, none of which by themselves matched the scopes of the books to which they were assigned, increased in frequency.

When David J. Haykin became the first chief of the library's newly created Subject Cataloging Division in 1949, he immediately took measures to reverse the deteriorating situation; and it was due in no small part to his efforts that striking changes were made. Among the latter were a more strict adherence to the use of conventional subject names rather than resorting too easily to subdivided headings, the employment of greater numbers of subject specialists in order to deal more adequately with a rising number of special subjects, an increase in the annual number of new subject headings, better provisions for the dissemination of subject heading additions and changes to the general cataloging community, and, finally, publication of the first reasonably useful and extensive description of subject heading practice written since Cutter's *Rules*—Haykin's *Subject Headings, a Practical Guide*.

One might reasonably assume that by means of such measures the goals of user convenience might have had some chance of being met. Certainly, this goal seems to have been squarely on Haykin's mind. User convenience, which he spoke of in his manual as the idea of "the reader as the focus," was in Haykin's opinion the most fundamental principle of subject heading work. Furthermore, Haykin provided even greater forcefulness to the concept by going well beyond user categorization based on the simplistic notion of broad types of libraries. In place of that earlier approach, he called for the more precise identification of the actual social groups that a library served and for making the dominant group or groups thus identified the basis for user convenience. In short, subject headings should be made with the actual group (or groups) of users that a library served in mind, regardless of the library's particular type. That user identification being accomplished, all subject heading decisions—those related to the degree of the specificity needed, those related to syntax, etc.—should be made carefully on a case-by-case basis in order to make the catalog as user convenient as possible.

Haykin's goal of making subject catalogs user convenient in terms of the distinct social groups that libraries served was not only an admirable goal but also served in many respects to bring subject cataloging back full circle to ideas that had been expressed nearly fifty years earlier. Hitchler, Crawford, and others had suggested that user convenience required that subject catalogers attempt to find out how users actually think in the subject searching process. Haykin's concept of the reader as the focus also stressed the same objective. With Haykin's thorough appeal to the idea, however, one also comes face to face with its contradictory nature. First, Haykin freely admitted that solid evidence for reader's habits in subject searching even in terms of groups was not really available. What was available were librarians' casual opinions about how users searched for subjects. But opinions of that kind constituted little more than the inconclusive kind of evidence that Crawford had discovered so many years earlier. Second, in the absence of any solid evidence of what users do in fact do in subject searching, regardless of whether they do so individually or in terms of groups, the actual decisions that have been based on such appeals (of which Haykin as well as those who have succeeded him at the Library have made in abundance) also have little objective basis. In fact, one may reasonably conclude that decisions made on that basis serve as much to rationalize past practice, as for any other need. Last, despite the glowing and enthusiastic way Haykin spoke of the necessity of providing for user convenience, he seems not to have been aware of the logical contradiction between that goal and still another goal that he strongly promoted and which has come to occupy an increasingly powerful role in the broader subject cataloging community since his time. The latter goal is the necessity to achieve subject access economically by means of centralized and cooperative cataloging—in this case through the use of Library of Congress subject headings in the forms of both its standardized list of headings and its subject cataloging copy. User convenience based on the dominant group or groups served by a particular library implied that the subject heading needs of each local library will vary significantly from those of other libraries and from those of the Library of Congress itself, at least to the extent that they vary from the dominant groups they serve. Thus, unless the local library serves users that match or nearly match those that are served by the Library of Congress, user convenience will not be served.

OBSERVATIONS

Appeals to user categories of the kind discussed here continue to be made and, in fact, are not confined to subject catalogers. They have been used, for example, in discussions of reference work and of bibliographical instruction as a way of showing how those two kinds of activities differ among different types of users. User categories of this kind appear to this author as a legacy of questionable worth, however, especially when they are used as a way to approach information retrieval patterns among users.

One aspect of such categorization that seems questionable is the conclusion expressed more than once over several decades that there are two kinds of users—specialists and general users—and that these groups are so distinct that they require essentially different kinds of subject access tools and, for that matter, different kinds of a wide variety of library service activities designed to help them find information. The questionable nature of this conclusion lies not so much in the concept of specialists as in the general user category. Most descriptions of the general user category express little more than the idea that general users are the opposite of specialists. They are, in effect, non-specialists. But characterizing general users as non-specialists makes the group into a moot category because that characterization says nothing about how general users actually do search for information. Even when attempts have been made to describe this category in a more positive way, however, the results have been equally dissatisfying because little more has been concluded of general users than a general disparagement of their intellectual abilities. On the basis of some descriptions of general users, in fact, one may reasonably wonder whether general users have mental processes that function at all. All of this leads to the question of whether there is any such real category as the general user. Furthermore, even if the existence of such a category could be demonstrated, it seems doubtful if it would provide anything in the way of a predictive basis upon which to construct information access tools and services.

The foregoing observation about the general user category is actually only an element of a second and far greater problem associated with user categorization. That problem is the questionable nature of devising user categories on the basis of social factors that are only accidentally related to the main concern of information access—that is, how the mental activities of users function in the information seeking process. What, for example, does the size or type of library that a user frequents really say about how users actually search for subjects, or use reference tools, or perform any of a variety of tasks associated with their library activity? It is entirely possible, of course, that in some particular instances, a correlation might be observed. To turn the observation around, however, and use it as a way to characterize the users of all libraries of any one size or type is not only supercilious but has a debilitating aspect as well because it easily leads to the specter of treating users in a presumptive fashion in which one simply assumes that the unfounded assumptions about the user category in question are true of the actual patrons who walk through the library door.

A far better approach to the matter of determining how to base decisions for making information retrieval tools or service that are user convenient is to observe, study and categorize use, not users. One reason for this seems obvious. Library patrons regularly display differing patterns of use depending on the information searching situation in which they find themselves. Specialists, for example, do not always search as specialists, and even when they do they may proceed in strikingly different patterns of information seeking behaviour depending on their information needs. Likewise, so-called general users often search as specialists in many particular instances, although their specialties may not in fact be those formally identified as special fields of literature or activity. This same line of reasoning may be applied to the whole range of users that are commonly placed in presumptive user categories.

A second reason for proceeding in this fashion is that it places users in a common arena based on their common intellectual habits rather than separating them into diverse categories based on what at best are only secondary social attributes. It is this view of users, in fact, that is so striking about Cutter's approach to the public in the last century. Cutter did not first separate users by some social distinction such as the size or type of library they frequented and then characterize the use in each of those categories. Instead, he began with a single public, divided its use patterns into a single continuum of behaviour, and then observed that behaviour in libraries. For him, all users' minds functioned in the same way, although not with the same efficiency or result. On that basis, Cutter was then able to design and rationalize a common system of subject access for all.

Cutter's use descriptions were based on an early hypothetical view of how the human mind functions, of course, and the applicability of that view would be a questionable starting point for the same effort today. But his approach does point out an important issue. If librarians begin with the idea that because users differ in social characteristics, their mental processes also differ in some absolute way, then they have logically excluded the possibility that the same information access tools may be made convenient to each group. That appears to be what has caused the opinion that the dictionary subject catalog is an imprecise tool useful only for general users rather than also for specialists. If, on the other hand, users are viewed as having common mental processes, there is then some possibility that such tools (and services as well) might be designed with an eye to being useful for the entire range of users in a useful and predictable fashion.

REFERENCES

1. The substance of this paper is taken from Francis Miksa, *The Subject in the Dictionary Catalog from Cutter to the Present* (Chicago: ALA, 1983) where the topic of user considerations is discussed in much greater detail but is scattered throughout a much longer text as a subsidiary theme. The documentation of the topic in that work is repeated here only sparingly.

2. Charles A. Cutter, *Rules for a Dictionary Catalog*, 4th ed (Washington, D.C.: U.S. Government Printing Office, 1904), p. 74.

3. David J. Haykin, *Subject Headings, a Practical Guide* (Washington, D.C.: U.S. Government Printing Office, 1951), p. 7.

4. Paul S. Dunkin, "Cataloging and the CCS: 1957-1966," *Library Resources and Technical Services* 11 (Summer 1967): 286.

5. The term "dictionary subject catalog" is used in place of the more awkward statement, "the subject element of the dictionary catalog." It is preferred to "subject headings," which does not convey the idea of a catalog system, and to "subject heading system," which does not identify the kind of catalog in which the system is found. There is no such separate thing as the dictionary subject catalog, of course.

6. *The Subject in the Dictionary Catalog*, pp. 37-44, 58-61, 72-86, and 126-43.

7. Charles A. Cutter, "Library Catalogues," *Public Libraries in the United States of America, their History, Condition and Management; Special Report, Part I* (Washington: U.S. Government Printing Office, 1876), p. 541.

8. Ibid., p. 530.

9. Cutter, *Rules for a Dictionary Catalog*, 4th ed. p. 79.

10. *The Subject in the Dictionary Catalog*, pp. 158-77, 204-211.

11. For the role of specialists, see Alexandra Oleson and John Voss (eds.), *The Organization of Knowledge in Modern America, 1860-1920* (Baltimore: Johns Hopkins University Press, 1979), especially chapters by John Higham, Edward Shils, and John Y. Cole.

12. *The Subject in the Dictionary Catalog*, pp. 178-79, 236-53.

13. Wayne Wiegand, *The Politics of an Emerging Profession: the American Library Association, 1876-1917* (Forthcoming).

14. Theresa Hitchler, *Cataloging for Small Libraries*, A.L.A. Publishing Board, Library Handbook, no. 2 (Boston: A.L.A. Publishing Board, 1905), p. 8.

15. Esther Crawford, "A.L.A. Subject Headings," *Library Journal* 32 (October 1907): 435-36; (November 1907): 500-1; (December 1907): 560-61.

16. Mary J. Briggs, "The A.L.A. List of Subject Headings," *Bulletin of the A.L.A.* 6(July 1912): 227-31.

17. *The Subject in the Dictionary Catalog*, pp. 256-73.

18. Ibid., pp. 284-91, 295-304.

19. Ibid., pp. 258-63; Elva S. Smith, *Subject Headings for Children's Books in Public Libraries and in Libraries in Elementary and Junior High Schools. . .* (Chicago: ALA, 1933)

20. Julia Pettee, *Subject Headings: The History and Theory of the Alphabetical Subject Approach to Books* (New York: H. W. Wilson Co., 1946), chs. 5-6.

21. *The Subject in the Dictionary Catalog*, pp. 304-8, 332-40, 364-82.

Where Have All the Moonies Gone?

Sanford Berman

According to the Good Book, Chapter 24, Verse 1: "Enter a corporate body directly under the name by which it is predominantly identified. . . . Determine the form of name of a corporate body from items issued by that body in its language. . ."[1] Doubtless, Library of Congress (LC) catalogers faithfully and properly applied that rule when constructing corporate name-forms—which, incidentally, also serve as subject headings—for Lech Walesa's now-banned labor federation and Reverend Moon's religious organization. That is, they must have examined materials produced in the home language—Polish and Korean—and determined the "predominant" form of name in each language. So, instead of "Solidarity," we find in MARC and CIP entries, "SNZZ 'Solidarnosc.' " And, rather than "Unification Church," we get "Segye Kidokkyo T'ongil Sillyong Hyophoe." Let's call these Exhibit A.

In June 1982, Temple University Press issued a 521-page, triple-column anthology, *Alternative Papers*,[2] containing about 200 reprinted articles arranged into 11 sections:

—The Press
—Nukes
—Appropriate Technology
—Third World
—Corporate Connections
—Repression
—Women
—Lesbians & Gay Men
—Work
—Organizing
—The Movement

Sanford Berman is Head Cataloger, Hennepin County Library, Edina, MN.

© 1984 by The Haworth Press, Inc. All rights reserved.

What would seem a decent minimum of subject tracings? Perhaps RADICALISM, SOCIAL MOVEMENTS, and SOCIAL CHANGE? Maybe also THIRD WORLD, NUCLEAR POWER, FEMINISM, GAYS (or GAY LIBERATION MOVEMENT), and ALTERNATIVE PRESS PUBLICATIONS—EXCERPTS?[3] What subject tracings did it actually get? None. Nada. Zip. Nichts. Call that Exhibit B.

At a Twin Cities' conference in late 1982, people like Harlan Cleveland, Tony Carbo Bearman, Paul Zurkowski, and Anita Schiller talked about "information as a resource and commodity," particularly discussing the merits and possible implications of the NCLIS Task Force report on private sector/public sector responsibilities.[4] During that weekend event, certain notable themes or topics recurred:

—FEE-BASED INFORMATION SERVICES
—GOVERNMENT PUBLISHING POLICY
—INFORMATION INDUSTRY
—INFORMATION POLICY
—INFORMATION SOCIETY
—TELEMATICS

Most libraries have material on those subjects. The Awful Truth, though, is that in most libraries such material cannot be identified nor retrieved through the catalog by means of those terms. Because they haven't been validated yet as nationally-acceptable headings by LC. That's Exhibit C.

In 1982, Little, Brown published what the jacket blurb described as an "adventure-filled memoir" by Robert MacNeil, co-host of PBS' *MacNeil-Lehrer Report*. Titled *The Right Place at the Right Time*, the work was classed in 813.54—i.e., contemporary American fiction—and accordingly got no subject headings.[5] Make that Exhibit D.

As Exhibit E: Marilyn Sachs' juvie novel, *Call Me Ruth*, appeared in 1982 (published by Doubleday). The jacket says: "A warm and moving story about the struggles of a young Jewish immigrant in New York City at the turn of the century." And the first page of text includes these passages:

> In the old country, my name was Rifka and my mother's name was Faigel. But when we came to America, I became Ruth and

my mother became Fanny. . . . Mamma was standing barelegged in the water, her skirts hiked up around her waist, rinsing off the large, white Passover tablecloth, for the holiday had just ended.

Okay. THIS is the annotation supplied by LC's juvenalia catalogers:

The daughter of a Russian immigrant family, newly arrived in Manhattan in 1908, has conflicting feelings about her mother's increasingly radical union involvement.

And this is the first—and only ethnic-related—subject tracing: RUSSIAN AMERICANS—FICTION.[6]

Well, the "exhibits" could continue to "Z" and beyond. The object in this litany of error and omission should be fairly transparent: to weaken confidence in centrally-performed cataloging and standard cataloging tools. Not for any personal nor mean-minded reasons, but simply because the fact is that our national cataloging products and services can't be completely trusted and should not be accepted automatically or uncritically by anyone who genuinely believes that cataloging should make material *more* rather than *less* accessible and retrievable.

To become more systematic: these are three basic principles that ought to underpin cataloging:

- *Intelligibility:* The catalog format, entry-elements, and terminology should make sense, should be understandable not just by staff, but also by ordinary patrons.
- *Findability:* Ideally, searchers should be able to "hit" what they want, especially when subject searching or author-browsing, on the first try.
- *Fairness:* Various *kinds* of materials—like print-AV and adult-juvenile—should be treated equitably; subject nomenclature should be unbiased; subject coverage should be fullsome, especially for women's, ethnic, sexual, political, and age-connected materials; and individual works deserve accurate representation, together with maximum accessibility.

Now, with those principles as a basis for evaluation, here's what's "wrong"—that is, dysfunctional and unhelpful—in currently-practiced descriptive and subject cataloging:

DESCRIPTIVE CATALOGING

Choice-of-entry

The new rules mandate entry of story or essay collections under title, rather than under editor or compiler.[7] So *Before the Golden Age: a Science Fiction Anthology of the 1930s,* compiled by Isaac Asimov, would be main-entried under "Before." Does that really make any difference? It does. Both studies and personal observation strongly suggest that people look for a *name* associated with a given work, not the title, and that they don't make fine distinctions between monographs and edited collections.[8] The practical effect of this AACR2 rule is to dictate shelf-location among the "Bs" instead of "As," where fiction-browsers might reasonably be looking for "Asimov" items. And in single-entry catalogs, the title would be the *sole* entry point.

Punctuation/Abbreviations

While not wishing to re-hash earlier debates, it still needs to be said that typical library users do not comprehend what "[s.1.]" or "[s.n.]" means, and that a significant number of users and staff alike plainly don't understand such cherished, long-standing bibliographic conventions as "min.," "b&w," "pt.," "in.," "b." (for "born"), "1." (for "leaves"), "d." (for "died"), "v.," "tr.," and "c" (for "copyright"). A 1979 Hennepin County Library survey strongly supported this.[9] And an earlier study regarding AV-abbreviations, conducted among Wisconsin college and high school students, did likewise.[10] If these sorts of data are important enough to include in a catalog entry, then they're important enough to be made comprehensible.

Notes

Non-archival libraries don't need some standard notes like "Includes index" or "Includes bibliography." However, other sorts of notes could prove extremely useful in helping potential readers decide whether they truly want a particular item, but these are less frequently supplied. For instance, HCL catalogers added this note to the record for Gloria Kaufman's *Pulling Our Own Strings: Feminist Humor and Satire:* "Includes anecdotes, songs, cartoons, poetry, essays, jokes, and comic routines." And they regularly make notes about sequels and cycles; e.g., "The 2d volume of the author's Dirshan The God-Killer saga, the 1st of which is The Lerious mecca, the 3d, Sword for the empire, and the 4th, The maneaters of Cascalon." Further, "Includes more than 50 photos, some in color, and over 70 traditional designs and projects to piece by machine and quilt in your lap." seems more likely to aid erstwhile borrowers than LC's cryptic collation for the same work:[11] "ill. (some col.)."

Added Entries

While not explicitly prohibited by the rules, a variety of helpful added entries simply don't get made—unless they're done locally. At HCL, for example, public service staff and patrons appreciate added entries for small, alternative, and regional presses, for notable people who contribute forewords or prefaces, for translators and illustrators, and for professional or community groups associated with a given work. Also, HCL catalogers routinely make title added entries for pieces of titles or rearranged titles *if* there's cause to believe that people might seek that entry-point. To illustrate: the orthodox title tracing for Wayne Dyer's 1976 best-seller, *Your Erroneous Zones*, was purely for "Your," filing in the Ys. But HCL made another for what may be the much more memorable permuted title: "Erroneous zones," filing in the Es.[12]

Form-of-heading #1

The "Solidarity" and "Unification Church" cases nicely exemplify this kind of dysfunctional rule. Nobody will score a "first hit" because nobody will look first under "SNZZ" or "Segye." And many libraries, for whatever reason, will not have introduced cross-references from the sensible forms to the *in*sensible ones, so the material may be permanently hidden and irretrievable. Obviously, either the rule should be revised to mandate name-establishment according to the predominant form in the language of the country where the material is being cataloged[13] or, paraphrasing George Orwell, a caution should appear in boldface at the bottom of every AACR2 page: **BREAK ANY OF THESE RULES SOONER THAN CREATE AN OUTRIGHT BARBAROUS ENTRY.**

Form-of-heading #2

AACR2 Rule 22.2C (p. 351) belatedly, but justly, liberated Sholem Aleichem, Orwell, Moravia, Celine, and Stendhal from a kind of bibliographic imprisonment, a confinement under the "real" names that they hadn't actually used when writing and that most readers wouldn't easily recognize, much less search for, in a catalog or on the shelves. This is Rule 22.2C1:

> If all the works by a person appear under one pseudonym, or if the person is predominantly identified in reference sources by one pseudonym, choose the pseudonym. If the real name if known, make a reference from the real name to the pseudonym.

That departure from the "real name" tradition represented a genuine improvement in catalog access and credibility. Indeed, it was a significant step toward demystification. (Why, for so many years, did the profession insist that patrons look under "Rabinowitz" or "Blair" or "Pincherle" or "Destouches" or "Beyle" when only "Aleichem," "Orwell," "Moravia," "Celine" and "Stendhal" appeared on title pages, on covers, on spines, on dust jackets, in reviews, and in bibliographies?) If Rule 22.2C1 ("One pseudonym") may be rightly regarded as a great advance, Rule 22.2C2—nestled just below it (p. 351-2)—cannot. Captioned "Predominant name," it reads:

> If the works of a person appear under several pseudonyms (or under the real name and one or more pseudonyms), choose one of those names if the person has come to be identified predominantly by that name in later editions of his or her works, or in other reference sources (in that order of preference). Make references from the other names.

The practical outcome of this instruction is that while novels in the Lavette Family saga by Howard Fast are expectably and properly entered under "Fast, Howard" and therefore shelved among the Fs, the Masao Masuto mysteries by E. V. Cunningham (a Fast pseudonym) are *also* entered under "Fast, Howard" and similarly shelved among the Fs. How come? Presumably because the author has written *more* works as "Fast" than as "Cunningham." The name form (and consequent shelf-location) thus derives from mathematics, not from common sense or utility. And the result is just as foolish and dysfunctional as the earlier "real name" practice. It could, of course, have been obviated if the rule-makers had merely validated the principle of "title-page cataloging."[14]

SUBJECT CATALOGING

One aspect of the subject cataloging problem is assignment practice, demonstrated by the *Alternative Papers* and *Call Me Ruth* examples. To *Alternative Papers* LC catalogers applied no vocabulary, and to *Call Me Ruth* they applied the wrong vocabulary. Still another defect inheres in LC assignment-policy regarding fiction, poetry, essays, humor, drama, and letters. Rarely, apart from adult anthologies and children's books, do such literary works get either topical or genre headings. (Robin MacNeil's richly-thematic memoir almost certainly went headingless due to its mistaken classification as "Fiction," an error that probably stemmed from cataloging "front matter' instead of the book itself during the CIP process.)[15] But school and public libraries, in particular, could greatly benefit from precisely such subject access to individual novels, plays, and other literature.[16]

While there's much to complain about concerning assignment, the vocabulary itself probably constitutes the largest part of the subject cataloging malaise. To begin with, too many active, primary headings remain awkward, archaic, or unfamiliar. They are terms not likely to be "first" sought by catalog users. For example:

LC form	*Common form*
AERONAUTICS—ACCIDENTS	AIRPLANE ACCIDENTS
ATOMIC WEAPONS AND DISARMAMENT	NUCLEAR DISARMAMENT
CARGO SHIPS—PASSENGER TRAVEL	FREIGHTER TRAVEL
CLOTHING, COLD WEATHER	WINTER CLOTHING
DWELLINGS	HOUSES
INFORMAL SECTOR (ECONOMICS)	UNDERGROUND ECONOMY

MICROMYS MINUTUS	HARVEST MOUSE
MILITARY SERVICE, COMPULSORY	DRAFT
MOVING PICTURE INDUSTRY—COLLECTIBLES	FILM COLLECTIBLES
NEAR EAST	MIDDLE EAST
ORTHODOX EASTERN CHURCH, GREEK	GREEK ORTHODOX CHURCH
PARENTING—RELIGIOUS ASPECTS—CHRISTIANITY	CHRISTIAN PARENTING
TRADE UNIONS	LABOR UNIONS

Secondly, a number of palpably biased or inauthentic descriptors persist in standard thesauri. MAN has not yet been transmuted into HUMANS. Alien ethnonyms still denote the Inuit and Saame. And neither JEWISH QUESTION nor YELLOW PERIL have been reformed or replaced.[17]

Thirdly, and most critical, is a continuing failure to promptly recognize and legitimize new topics, as well as finally validating "old" ones. Among the "old":

> BROWN LUNG DISEASE
> CLASSICAL MUSIC[18]
> CREATIONISM
> DRAFT REGISTRATION
> FAMILY PLANNING
> HOME REMEDIES
> HUMAN SERVICES
> INTEREST RATES
> MARXISM
> NEW LEFT
> PARTICIPATORY MANAGEMENT
> POLLUTION CONTROL

And among the "new":

> ANTI-PORNOGRAPHY MOVEMENT
> APPROPRIATE TECHNOLOGY
> "BABY BOOM" GENERATION
> CHRISTIAN BROADCASTING

DIVORCE MEDIATION SERVICES
HOMOPHOBIA
HOSPICES
NEW AGE
NEW FEDERALISM
NEW RIGHT
NUCLEAR FREEZE CAMPAIGN
PAY EQUITY
SAGEBRUSH REBELLION
SMALL BUSINESS LOANS
STARCH-BLOCKER DIET
TUITION TAX CREDIT
VIDEO DISPLAY TERMINALS
VIOLENCE AGAINST WOMEN
WELLNESS LIFESTYLE

If it's agreed that at least some of these things are really "wrong" with cataloging—and we take cataloging seriously—what's to be done? Well, there's no instant "fix." For instance, replacing LC subject headings with another system, like PRECIS, won't miraculously make subject cataloging "work." In fact, the same people would be applying and developing the new system who made a mess out of the old one. And the impact on existing subject catalogs could easily be disastrous. Nor is there a technological "fix." Merely changing from a card to an online catalog doesn't automatically change the *content* of the cataloging nor will it fully compensate for the lack of a good, modern, controlled vocabulary and user-oriented descriptive data. So what then? It may be hard medicine, but we *can* do two things, "inside" and "outside."

Outside: If we can identify a product or policy that's not working but can be repaired, we should let the responsible parties know about it. With respect to that "Solidarity" rule, it would be a matter of communicating—either individually or through professional groups—with the appropriate LC office and ALA committee. It's most effective to precisely specify what's wrong—and propose a remedy. (That goes for subject headings, too.) And it would be wise to publicize your communications in the library press. The more publicity, the more leverage, and the greater chance of getting things changed.

Inside: While admittedly tougher, given staff and money cuts everywhere, it's a matter of critically examining—and, when necessary, altering—"outside copy," as in the Robin MacNeil case. It's a matter of locally creating and assigning subject headings when you need them.[19] And it's a matter of trying to perform as much catalog maintenance as possible, especially adding essential cross-references between subject and name forms.[20]

To sum up: The Moonies haven't gone anywhere. It only seems that way. Which is lamentable. But also correctible.

NOTES

1. The "Good Book": *Anglo-American Cataloguing Rules*. 2d ed. (Chicago: American Library Association, 1978). For "Basic Rule" 24.1, see p. 402.
2. Edited by Elliott Shore, Patricia J. Case, and Laura Daly.
3. Except that LC employs UNDERDEVELOPED AREAS, ATOMIC ENERGY, and HOMOSEXUALS instead of THIRD WORLD, NUCLEAR POWER, and GAYS. ALTERNATIVE PRESS PUBLICATIONS, of course, would be an altogether new heading.
4. *Public Sector/Private Sector Interaction in Providing Information Services: Report to the NCLIS* (Washington, DC: GPO, 1982).
5. The error has since been corrected. The current MARC record shows the title is classed in PN 4874 and 070.924 (biographies of journalists).
6. For more on how LC mis-cataloged this work, see my "'Jewish Question' in Subject Cataloging (Continued)," *Technicalities*, v. 3, no. 1 (Jan. 1983), p. 9, and v. 3, no. 3 (March 1983), p. 6.
7. See AACR2 Rule 21.1C, p. 286.
8. See, for instance, Phyllis A. Richmond, "The AACR, Second Edition, What Next?," in Maurice J. Freedman and S. Michael Malinconico, editors, *The Nature and Future of the Catalog* (Phoenix: Oryx Press, 1979), p. 192-3.
9. See Larry Legus, "Sure, They Save Space, But Who Knows What They Mean?" *HCL Cataloging Bulletin*, no. 40 (May/June 1979), p. 24-9.
10. Jane Schlueter and Robert D. Little, "The Mystery of Ips and Mono; Or, Do Students Understand AV Card Catalog Terms?" *Wisconsin Library Bulletin*, Nov./Dec. 1973, p. 381-3.
11. The work: *Lap quilting with Georgia Bonesteel* (Oxmoor House, 1982).
12. For more on title added entries, see my "Title Access: the Need, the Policy, and the Practice," *Technicalities*, v. 1, no. 1 (Dec. 1980), p. 6-7; Janet Swann Hill, "Letters to the editor," *ibid.*, v. 1, no. 2 (Jan. 1981), p. 2; my response to Hill, *ibid.* v. 1, no. 4 (1981), p. 2; and my "Missing Titles," *ibid.*, v. 2, no. 3 (March 1982), p. 11.
13. On March 24, 1983, at the PLA National Conference in Baltimore, I made this "action-recommendation" to the Cataloging Needs of Public Libraries Committee: Replace the 2d paragraph of Rule 24.1 ("Determine the form of name of a corporate body from items issued by that body in its language. . .") with: "Determine the form of name of a corporate body from items issued by or about that body in the language of the country where those items are being cataloged, provided that the translation is a true rendering of the original name."
14. The principle can still be fully validated by means of this proposal, also made in Baltimore: "Compress Rules 22.2C1 (One Pseudonym), 22.2C2 (Predominant name), and 22.2C3 (No predominant name) into a single instruction: If the works of a person appear under one pseudonym, under several pseudonyms, or under the real name and one or more pseudonyms, enter each work under the name specifically associated with it, making references from and to the person's other names."

15. This continuing situation prompted another Baltimore suggestion: Institute stringent quality control at the Library of Congress, ensuring that LC catalogers and classifiers work from substantial, if not full, galleys rather than frequently misleading and inaccurate "front matter." See also my "Time to Blow the Whistle on CIP," *Technicalities*, v. 3, no. 4 (April 1983), p. 6.

16. For more on theory and methods, see my "Reference, Readers and Fiction: New Approaches," *Reference Librarian*, nos. 1/2 (Fall/Winter 1981), p. 45-53, later updated in "Fiction Access," *Technicalities*, v. 2, no. 7 (July 1982), p. 7, 16.

17. For further discussion, examples, and sourcelists, see my *Prejudices and Antipathies* (Metuchen, NJ: Scarecrow Press, 1971); "Access/Equity," in *Joy Of Cataloging* (Phoenix: Oryx Press, 1981), p. 61-155; and "Where Have All The Women Gone?," *Technicalities:* v. 2, no. 12 (Dec. 1982), p. 15; v. 3, no. 1 (Jan. 1983), p. 10; v. 3, no. 2 (Feb. 1982), p. 11.

18. Randall W. Scott addressed the "classical music" issue in "Sour Notes," *Technicalities*, v. 2, no. 4 (April 1982), p. 9.

19. For aids and ideas, see "Do-It-Yourself Subject Cataloging: Sources and Tools," *Library Journal*, April 15, 1982, p. 785-6, later updated in *Technicalities:* v. 2, no. 6 (June 1982), p. 8; v. 2, no. 8 (Sept. 1982), p. 7.

20. In some catalogs, for instance, material is subject traced under either NEAR EAST or MIDDLE EAST—i.e., *both* terms appear in the catalog—but there's no link, no connection, made between the two sequences.

Classification Schemes as Cognitive Maps

Richard A. Gray

Catalogers and classifiers generate an intellectual instrument whose use devolves on others. They devise classification schemes, modify them when the need for revision becomes manifest, monitor them, maintain and apply them to a vast array of discrete specimens of intellectual workmanship, books. This entire labor is then entrusted to reference librarians to apply in practice in an existential mode, a librarian-in-the-real-world mode, in response to queries like "Where are your books on Polynesian ethnology, computer technology and languages, anorexia nervosa, the Shakespearean sonnet, rock music, and the Secretary of the Interior, Mr. James Watt."

So close is the relationship between classifiers and reference librarians that the word "interaction" may well be felt too limp in lexical precision. I suspect that the *mot juste* is not "interaction" but rather "synergism." The biological idea that "one cannot exist without the other" provides the essential clue to an understanding of the ambivalent ambience of reference librarian and classifier. Synergistic ambivalence accurately invokes an image of love and hate, of hate in love, and love in hate. The word "interaction" does not have anything like this kind of connotative power.

I do not endorse ambivalence as such. In fact, I wish it did not exist. A wise library administrator once told me that if he had a free hand, he would dissolve the technical versus public services dichotomy. According to this utopian vision there would be only librarians who would divide their time, in some equible measure, between cataloging and classifying and reference work.

Richard A. Gray is librarian, Business Department, Rockford Public Library, Rockford, IL.

This kind of "if I were king" vision is utopian. Everything in the modern complex world militates against dreams of rationality. The socio-economic world of today demands ever increasing orchestrations of the "division of labor" for dividing labor into increasingly precisely defined categories is thought to promote efficiency, and efficiency is the implacable god of the Twentieth Century before whom we must all make obeisance. Though we must obey the god, we should also inform this divinity that obedience exacts a fearsome price. The price includes the love-hate ambivalence referred to above which in turn derives from the brute fact that those who devise, modify, and maintain classification schemes are a different group of people from those who use them existentially, with living and increasingly befuddled patrons.

Library classification schemes are cognitive maps by which librarians and library patrons plot their present positions and plan their horizontal and vertical movements within a database; the database being in this instance a library's total collections. Like physical maps, cognitive maps need fixed points of reference such as the cardinal points of the compass, indicators of altitude and of scale. With respect to the basic elements of design in map-making, innovation is not permitted; for if it were, both position and movement would be fatally compromised. Applying the map analogy to library classification schemes means that here too we must require fixity of reference points for if they are allowed to become muted or blurred, then the precision and finesse with which anyone can read the cognitive map of a library classification scheme would diminish markedly. That there has occurred a sad falling off in the clarity of the cognitive map which is the scheme known as *Dewey* or *DDC* is demonstrable. One has only to read the published plaints of DDC's critics to know that the natives are decidedly restless if not yet openly rebellious. See in particular Berman,[1] and virtually every issue of the *Unabashed Librarian*. It is of the utmost importance that the critic of the venerable *Dewey* state precisely what changes have been effected in the schema in recent years and over recent editions and in what degree these transformations may be reconcilable with the canons of a properly expedient classificatory logic. If we conceive a classification scheme as a cognitive mapping of a universal database, then we can characterize the *Dewey* map as exhibiting certain fixed cartographic reference points among which, at the very least, the following must be allowed. In *Dewey* the effable universe is "decimated" or divided into tenth segments each of which is infinitely divisible decimally. These tenth segments of the knowable universe are then enchained as linked classes of inter-connected and semi-autonomous knowledge.

In light of the tortured revisions introduced by Dewey's latter-day disciples which contravene the categories of his classificatory thought, an explication of the Dewey scheme as Dewey conceived it is essential.

Dewey's scheme was decimal, hierarchical and contextual. It assumed a chain of inter-connected, semi-autonomous classes of human knowledge ranging from generalia (the 000s) to the 900s which celebrate the glories and follies of the Lords of Creation, Homo Sapiens. Following Dewey's sequential logic, it is obvious that before we can properly consider the chronological record of man as a builder of time-dependent cultures, we must enter into a sympathetic appreciation of what sapient man must do to create the cultures that can become the focus of the chronicles of the 900s. There is first man confronting the uncertainties of himself, his mind, his psyche, the 100s. Next follows Dewey's recognition that man, the existential being, also confronts the inexplicable, the mysterious, the uncertainties of the previous class compounded to the nth degree; thus is Dewey's 200 class. Next Dewey has his homo sapiens look at himself in befuddlement if not in uncertainty. Here Dewey's "man" sees himself as a social, economic, and political animal and thus the 300s arise. The supreme mystery of language, far more mysterious than he in his pre-Chomskian era ever imagined it to be, Dewey placed in the 400s. Man's scientific explorations and investigations and the results thereof are classed in the 500s as a semi-autonomous domain which serves as the parent and source of the derivative kingdom of technology, the 600s in Dewey's schema. The fine arts and literature distribute themselves over the 700s and 800s while the scheme concludes with the celebration of man's own history in the 900s.

Simply reviewing the Dewey classes offers additional evidence, if we needed any, that a fine classificatory intelligence has been at work here. Dewey's scheme has an intrinsic elegance which is why it has always been attractive to theoreticians among librarians. By contrast the plodding pragmatism of LCC, bereft of Dewey's internal echoings, makes the latter appear to be just that, plodding pragmatism.

Fundamental to an understanding of Dewey as a classificatory philosopher was his insistence on the primacy of context as he made unmistakably clear in his first publication: "not only are all books on the subject sought, found together, but the most nearly allied subjects precede and follow, they in turn being preceded by other allied subjects as far as practicable."[2]

For Dewey the context of any book's primary focus was to govern that book's assigned classification number. Dewey was intransigent on this point and for as long as he lived and could control his system there occurred no divergence from contextual analysis as the pivotol premise of his system.

For many years the scheme because of its elegance and in spite of some crudities, proved to be as workable as anyone has any right to expect. But difficulties, contradictions, anomalies kept cropping up among which were some that cried out for reform and which were justly reformed. As Dewey left his scheme, cultural anthropology, ethnology, was classed in 572 where such writings nestled up to the biology of human evolution and primitive man, e.g., Neanderthal man. Dewey took the same unanthropological view of non-European cultures as Kipling did. They were "lesser breeds without the Law" and hence this flagrant ethnic chauvinism came to be enshrined in his classification scheme. It is now happily gone, thanks to a reform instigated by those who now control the scheme, following Dewey's death. The present stewards are Mr. John Comaromi and his staff in the Decimal Classification Office in the Library of Congress.

The criticisms that many have made of Dewey's schema appear to divide into two distinct groups: those formulated by practicing librarians who use DDC and those put forth by the custodians of the system. The quality of the criticisms differ sharply from one group to the other. My own plaints have reference to the inadequacy of DDC's capacity to make peace with, nay even to acknowledge, the disruptive demands of the Twentieth Century, that century which casts doubt on many presumed certitudes about which Dewey had no dubieties at all. He postulated an absolute dichotomy between the biological and social realms, his 500s and 300s respectively. The new field of sociobiology not only subverts Dewey's dichotomy but resists incorporation into his schema. Sociobiology as a fusion discipline is only the beginning of those modern studies which defy Dewey's overly neat divisions of the universal conceptual pie. Other disturbers of the scheme and of the conceptual peace are psychobiology, biomechanics, psycholinguistics, sociolinguistics, each of which, by a minimal interpretation suggests that Dewey's decimal sub-kingdoms were by no means as self-contained as he conceived them to be.

More critical than the classificatory reception of fusion disciplines such as these is the failure of the scheme to deal with the twentieth century's master revolution whose intermediate and remote consequences we are only now beginning to glimpse. The revolution is the computer and everything that that explosive word entails socially, economically, philosophically, even theologically. Computerology is as pervasive as I suggest because it is closely allied to the work that is going forward in artificial intelligence, optical character recognition and cognitive simulation. I call the model of artificial intelligence the master revolution of the twentieth century.[3] And how have recent editions of the post-Melvil Dewey *DDC* handled this revolution? The answer, I fear, does not reflect creditably on the logical acuity of Dewey's stewards.

If, in Sanford Berman style, one wished to indict a classificatory abberation, one could direct one's attention to the new DDC's fumbling of this question.

To begin, DDC shuffles artificial intelligence off to Dewey's sidelines, the 000s generalia, where it occupies the position of 001.535. It is important to note what generalia meant to Dewey. For him they comprised those studies which *in form* could be conceived as underlying and supporting all disciplines and studies; thus they comprehended general periodicals, encyclopedias, periodicals, bibliographies. For Dewey, generalia were publication forms, not subjects or disciplines.

Interpretations of generalia that have appeared in recent editions of *DDC* diverge radically from the Deweyan model. The placement of computer science, and its allied fields, in the 001s is placement in contextual isolation. By contextual isolation, I mean that these subjects of seminal importance are denied contiguity with the broader encompassing disciplines from which they derive. The modern *DDC*'s deficiencies in the disposition to isolate whole fusion studies appears glaringly when *DDC*'s numbers for such studies are contradistinguished from those used by LCC.

Where LCC classifies books on artificial intelligence and electronic computers, demonstrates LC's continuing commitment to embedding subjects in their most immediate contexts. In this system the cognitive map of total knowledge is not vitiated by ad hoc devices which uproot subjects from their proper embedded places in larger contexts of knowledge.

The laboriously revised modern *DDC*, at least the *DDC*'s of editions 16 through 19, have continuously had recourse to disruptive ad hoc devices whose cumulative effect is to blur the cognitive map of the Dewey data base.

In a letter addressed to me, dated November 18, 1982, John P. Comaromi of the Decimal Classification Office wrote: "For years we despaired at having the social side of public health in 614." He then adds: "We finally had an opportunity to rectify matters and did so."[4] Thus Comaromi and his colleagues "rectified" matters by moving the "social" side *as well as the scientific-technical side* of such subjects as food contamination and water pollution from 614s to an appallingly disruptive position in the 363s. I use the phrase "appallingly disruptive" because it forcefully encompasses the reaction of the traditional (and therefore older) Dewey-using reference librarian when he or she encounters evidences of Comaromi's "social sidism" in the stacks. What the revisers conspicuously fail to understand is that it is not just the "social" side of food contamination that is now being treated as a social science, but the scientific-technical underpinning of the subject as well. That many solid scientific texts are now being classified as though they were social science is demonstrable. To sustain my argument I believe it essential to make the demonstration.

I want to use two recently published books by way of illustration. They are *Food Safety*, edited by Howard R. Roberts,[5] and *Handbook of Nonpoint Pollution: Sources and Management* by Novotny and Chesters.[6] *Food Safety* is classed in 363.192 and the *Handbook* in 363.2394.

I postulate even now the process of classification as an intellectual enterprise presupposes that the analyst ask a few elementary questions such as: Who are the authors; What are their qualifications and affiliations; and What have they written? With respect to *Food Safety*, the answers are as follows: The authors and contributors are all holders of the PhD degree, probably in biochemistry; their institutional affiliations are impressive and impeccable, and what they have jointly written is an excellent state-of-the-art summary of the biochemistry of food contamination and adulteration. Even the most desultory sampling of the text will persuade the fair-minded reader that what we are dealing with here is a solid treatise in the biochemistry of foods, an understanding of which presupposes more than a casual education in the field. Only in the final chapter, which is also the briefest and least adequate chapter, does a contributor get around to considering, in a cursory manner, some issues relating to governmental regulation of the food industry. On the strength of these few brief and not especially illuminating remarks constituting less than one percent of the total text, has *Food Safety* been deemed to be a work in the social sciences despite the massive internal evidence that it is nothing of the kind. 363.192 for *Food Safety*, I can only call an example of a perverse misclassification.

Turning to the *Handbook of Nonpoint Pollution*, the answers to the indicated questions are: The authors are holders of the PhD degree; They hold professorships of civil engineering and soil science at prestigious American universities, and what they have jointly written is an abstruse treatise in hydrology, soil erosion and degradation, and groundwater pollution. Do not trouble to go to the *Handbook* unless you have very recently refurbished your mathematics and unless you are underpinned with a solid education in the physical sciences. Clearly, the *Handbook* is not the stuff that the social sciences are made of.

What are the effects of the aggrandizement of the social sciences and consequent impoverishment of the sciences which are clearly discernible in the modern *DDC*? They are many. First, there is annoyance, then a progressively increasing befuddlement; and as one examines the proferred justifications for recent dislocations in the schedules, there emerges a rage response at seeing Melvil Dewey's lifework set on its ears.

More than annoyance and rage are involved however. Far more importantly, there occurs an erosion of confidence in the mind of the reference librarian who is now no longer sure that he/she can read the Dewey map with speed and finesse. The cognitive map has begun to fade, to become hazy and to lack sharpness of definition. Answers to questions that formerly could have been rendered with dispatch and precision now have to be laboriously qualified.

Ultimately, and most regrettably there emerges a contempt in the mind of the reference librarian, a contempt for his/her basic classificatory instrument, the cognitive map itself.

The two books discussed above are illustrative only. Since the inauguration of classification under the mandated rules of DDC-19, scores, if not hundreds, of solid scientific texts have been sent off to graze aimlessly and irretrievably in the misty and murky realms of the social sciences. Though Comaromi asserts that only the "*social*" side of environmental science has been so relegated, this contention is, as we have seen, demonstrably in error. Both the "social" and the scientific "sides" of environmental science have now been dispatched to this barren pasture. I might add that this has been done in flagrant violation of what I take to be a necessary first premise of Deweyism, namely, that the context of any book's subject is sovereign, that it alone will determine that book's placement in Dewey's scheme. It does appear that modern DDC classifiers can no longer distinguish between scientific and social science writing. Distinctions which are manifest to unfettered intelligences are opaque to those who show an overwrought concern with the "social" side of science.

"When Change Is Not Necessary, It Is Necessary Not to Change." This quotation from Edmund Burke was given me by Comaromi,[7] who contended that the expressed attitude of philosophic conservatism aptly characterizes his own work as a reviser of Dewey's classification scheme. Although it is perhaps churlish to deny the validity of a man's self-assessment of philosophic position, regretfully I must do just that. Nothing in the record of recent revisions indicates that Comaromi's revisionary proposals were ever restrained by a deference to the Burkean commandment, which in paraphrase, can be construed as: Change nothing at all unless you can establish an iron-clad case for the necessity for change.

In fact, it is precisely the necessity for change which is most conspicuously lacking in recent, convulsive upheavals in the DDC schedules. On the contrary, changes which violate fundamental tenets of Dewey's thought have been introduced without regard for how they will affect front-line users and interpreters of the scheme, reference librarians.

I have used the analogy of a classification scheme as a cognitive map, and I want to close on the same theme. A map requires fixed, unvarying reference points if it is to be read with celerity, precision and finesse. The root assumptions of the scheme, such as the Deweyan premises of hierarchy and contextual analysis, must not be permitted to change. Since Comaromi has done so first, I will invoke Burke against him: precisely here is there a paramount necessity not to change.

The modern DDC is fraught with deep ambiguities of classificatory principle. The difficulties reference librarians experience in navigating with the faded Dewey map increase geometrically with each succeeding edition. I think it highly probable, therefore, that a consensus will emerge to declare that the process of ceaseless ad hoc revision must be brought to an end. At that point, it may become possible to begin to take Burke's conservatism seriously and to ask exactly where, and where not, does there exist a bona fide necessity for change.

REFERENCES

1. Sanford Berman, "DDC 19: An Indictment," *Library Journal*, 105:585-89 (1 March 1980).
2. Melvil Dewey, *Classification and Subject Index for Cataloging and Arranging the Books and Pamphlets of a Library*. Amherst, Massachusetts, 1876. p. 7.
3. The best, most succinct account of artificial intelligence known to me is: Hubert L. Drefus, *What Computers Can't Do: A Critique of Artificial Reason*. New York, Harper & Row, c1972. A later edition of this work has been published, not seen by the writer.
4. John P. Comaromi to Richard A. Gray, private correspondence.
5. *Food Safety*, edited by Howard R. Roberts. New York, Wiley, c1981. DDC class number 363.1'79 LCC class number TX531.F65
6. Novotny, Vladimir. *Handbook of Nonpoint Pollution*, by Vladimir Novotny and Gordon Chester. New York, Van Nostrand, c1981. DDC class number 363.7394, LCC class number TD423.N69. It is obvious that LCC, confining both of these titles to its "T" (technology) class, shows not the slightest concern for DDC's "social" side of environmental science.
7. Comaromi to Gray, private correspondence.

The DDC and Its Users: Current Policies

John A. Humphry
Judith Kramer-Greene

INTRODUCTION

In the article by Richard A. Gray, also included in this issue of *The Reference Librarian*,[1] questions are raised about certain policies and decisions regarding the preparation and application of the 19th edition of the Dewey Decimal Classification (DDC) and about changes and revisions which have been introduced in Editions 16 through 19. Such policies and decisions have an impact on the organization of libraries that use the system, the quality of service provided to users of these libraries, and—apropos of the relationship between reference and technical services—the work of reference librarians and others involved in public service.

The purpose of the DDC—and the editorial and advisory apparatus that supports the system—is to serve the needs of librarians who use the system. Therefore, when changes are made, users have every right to expect constructive changes. These are, in fact, the policies of the publisher of the DDC, Forest Press. That some librarians feel the publisher has not been entirely successful in implementing these policies is evident from several recent publications.[2] Nevertheless, efforts are made to respond to questions, suggestions, and criticisms when they are directed to the Editor of the

---

John A. Humphry is Executive Director of the Forest Press, and Judith Kramer-Greene is Editor of Forest Press publications. This article is based on material drawn from publications of the Press and discussions with John P. Comaromi, Editor of the DDC and Chief of the Decimal Classification Division of the Library of Congress. It was written with the assistance of Gordon Stevenson, Associate Editor of *The Reference Librarian*.

© 1984 by The Haworth Press, Inc. All rights reserved.

DDC, the publisher, or others involved in the production and maintenance of the system.

What follows is a description of the structure and organization of the various elements involved in preparing and editing the Classification, with particular attention paid to the interrelationships between the editorial process and the system's users. The reader should keep in mind that there are two factors that make the editing of the DDC a complicated and, at times, controversial task. First, there is the recognition by Forest Press, the organization to which the system has been entrusted, of its responsibility to the many libraries that use the system. Forest Press knows full well that editorial revision has far-reaching consequences. At the same time, the Press knows that a *lack* of editorial change may have equally far-reaching consequences, although of a different sort. The second fact to keep in mind is the awesome number of libraries that use the system. Problems are created not only by the size of this user population, but also by the great diversity of type of libraries. Before commenting on how the system responds to its users, however, we must first address the question, Who are the users of Dewey?

In 1977, Ingetraut Dahlberg estimated that the DDC is used by some 25,000 libraries throughout the world.[3] Current use based on sales would suggest a figure between 30,000 and 35,000 libraries. In addition to its use by librarians as a system for shelving books or organizing entries in classified catalogues, the DDC is widely used in printed national and other bibliographies. Use of the system on a worldwide scale has increased to the point where today it is utilized in more than 130 countries.

Outside of the English-speaking world, the use of the DDC has been facilitated by an increasing number of translations as well as by what the Press terms "adaptations." Translations are identified as adaptations when parts of the schedules are restructured to take into account local traditions and culture, an essential process if the international editions are to be of practical use. The DDC has been translated into French, and adaptations have been prepared in Spanish and Hindi. Adaptations in Italian and Arabic are currently in preparation, and there are likely to be more of these in the coming decades. Here, we have noted only what may be identified as "official" translations and adaptations, those approved and monitored by Forest Press. There are many unofficial translations of DDC, or of parts of the DDC, in languages as diverse as Hebrew, Greek, Danish, Indonesian, Turkish, and Japanese.

CHANGE

The most difficult editorial questions involve what to change, when to change, and how to change. Two broad types of change must be dealt with. First, there are changes in the quantity and structure of knowledge. New topics emerge, old topics disappear, various topics are combined in interdisciplinary subjects. The problem here, obviously, is how to fit these changes into the existing system with as little disruption as possible, the purpose being to keep to a minimum the number of relocations that would require reclassification. The other category of change involves cases where for one reason or another, the present schedules are inadequate or outdated. The evolution of disciplines seems to be such that one cannot continue forever patching up an old system. There have emerged new paradigms and new relationships, and these parts of the schedules need to be completely rewritten.

Both types of change involve difficult decisions because of their enormous impact. On the one hand, if the DDC had not been reworked, it is unlikely it would have survived for over a century, nor would it have ever reached such wide international use. On the other hand, all those involved in the preparation of revisions and new editions are fully conscious of the problems change creates. They must balance the need for a more modern system against the disruptions and economic disadvantages of reclassification.

WHO MAKES MAJOR POLICY CHANGES?

The DDC is not in the public domain. It is owned and copyrighted by Forest Press, a nonprofit organization which is a division of the Lake Placid Education Foundation. In order to provide a continuous and responsible system for the development of policy and the advancement of the Classification, the Forest Press Committee was made the legal trustee of the Dewey heritage. In all matters relating to editing and publishing the DDC, the Forest Press Committee constitutes the highest level of policy formation. The day-to-day operations of Forest Press and the coordination of all matters related to the DDC both nationally and internationally are the responsibility of the Executive Director of Forest Press. The coordination of editorial activities regarding the development of the Classification is the responsibility of the Editor of the DDC. The current edition, the

19th, and the three previous editions were produced under the editorial direction of Benjamin A. Custer. Since 1980, John P. Comaromi has been the Editor. Although the Editor plays the central role in the editorial process, many others representing a wide spectrum of library users, contribute to the formation and execution of policies and practices.

THE EDITORIAL PROCESS

The following individuals and agencies contribute in various ways to revisions of the schedules and the development of new schedules.

The Editor and the Decimal Classification Division

The Decimal Classification Division is within the office of the Assistant Librarian of Congress for Processing Services. John P. Comaromi, who holds a joint appointment as Editor of the DDC and Chief of the Decimal Classification Division, and his staff perform two separate but related functions. They edit, revise, and compile the Schedules, Tables, and Index to the DDC, a function performed under a contractual agreement between Forest Press and the Library of Congress. The editorial staff also applies DDC class numbers to Library of Congress cataloguing records. In this way, classification theory and practice are combined, allowing for continuous and thorough editorial review and development, as well as for day-to-day testing of the scheme's validity. By working with the current literature, the Editor is in a position to see what classes should be added or changed on the basis of "literary warrant"; this process is fundamental to the progress of the system. Currently, around 100,000 books are classified annually by the Division, all of which are entered in the MARC records. To date, over two and a half million titles with DDC class numbers are in the MARC records.

The Decimal Classification Editorial Policy Committee (EPC)

Based on his continuous review of the Classification and its application, the Editor makes recommendations for changes, major and minor, to the Decimal Classification Editorial Policy Committee (EPC). The members of the EPC are nominated in alternate years (with overlapping terms of office) by the Forest Press Committee and by the Cataloging and Classification Section of the Resources and Technical Services Division of the American Library Association. They are appointed by the Trustees of the Lake Placid Education Foundation. Representing the users of the DDC, the EPC is made up of practicing librarians from various types of libraries as well as representatives from faculties of schools of library and information science. The EPC usually meets twice a year to discuss, analyze, and finally, to recommend to the Forest Press Committee those changes it deems necessary and useful to the library community. Recommendations by the EPC are a major factor in the formation of policy related to changes in the schedules, new editions, and the overall direction of the Classification. Although it is an advisory committee, no case comes to mind where its recommendations to the Forest Press Committee were not followed.

The Forest Press Committee

Members of the Forest Press Committee are appointed by the Lake Placid Education Foundation. One of its members represents the Foundation, and the other members are chosen from the ranks of professional librarians and library educators. The Forest Press Committee, which is the policy-making body for the Classification, meets at least twice a year to review EPC recommendations for change as well as production and fiscal matters.

Forest Press and the Executive Director

The Executive Director of Forest Press is the chief administrative officer responsible for carrying out the policies of the Forest Press Committee. He and his staff coordinate activities at the national and international level, and work closely with the Editor of the DDC on matters related to the development of the system. Forest Press, the publisher of the Classification, is located in Albany, New York.

Subject Analysis Committee

The Subject Analysis Committee (of the Cataloging and Classification Section of the ALA Resources and Technical Services Division) has in recent years held Dewey Hearings at annual and midwinter ALAs. The purpose of these Hearings is to disseminate information to the Dewey community and to encourage greater participation from Dewey users.

RESPONSES TO USERS' NEEDS

In addition to the organizations described above, Forest Press and the Decimal Classification Division respond to users' needs by providing a variety of helpful tools and services.

Perhaps the best known is the supplement entitled *DC&*, which provides a channel of communication between those who produce the Classification and those who use it. *DC&* is issued free of charge to purchasers of the unabridged edition. Since the release in 1979 of Edition 19, three issues of *DC&* have been published. The bulk of each issue is devoted to additions, corrections, and changes in the Classification. The remainder of the issue provides general information about the Press, the Division, and the Committees.

Another helpful tool for users is the recently published (1980) *Manual on the Use of the Dewey Decimal Classification: Edition 19*. The *Manual* goes a long way toward explaining Division practices and the reasons underlying these practices. Similar publications planned by the Division and Forest Press for future release are a *Beginners' Guide to the Use of the DDC*, and an atlas whose maps will display Dewey area numbers.

The release in 1982 of the *301–307 Sociology Expanded Version Based on Edition 19* exemplifies another kind of response to users' needs. The 301–307 schedule in Edition 19 was completely new in structure but was not sufficiently detailed to encompass the burgeoning number of publications in this area. Therefore, when the need became apparent, the Division undertook an expanded version of 301–307, which Forest Press made available free of charge to purchasers of Edition 19.

Another service provided by the Decimal Classification Division is the segmentation of Dewey numbers for dissemination by centralized services. The purpose of segmentation is to provide librarians with the option of broad or close classification, and to permit libraries of any size to abridge Dewey numbers to meet their specific needs.

The Proposed Revision of 780 Music was released in 1980. This publication represents a departure from traditional policy, for it is "proposed" only, which means librarians can examine the new schedule and comment on it before it is included, in whole or in part, in a future DDC. As stated in the Publisher's Foreword, "It is an attempt to permit classifiers and librarians, who have long recognized the need for a thoroughly revised music schedule for Dewey, to test its pragmatic value."[4]

In addition to these various publications, John P. Comaromi and members of his staff, with the help of Forest Press, have organized seminars and workshops around the country on the use of Edition 19. The first workshop took place in New York City on November 19, 1979, and a number have been given each year since then. The workshops have a practical orientation, allowing participants to test their knowledge and understanding of the Classification.

Finally, Forest Press is currently involved in a computer study which should be beneficial to Dewey users. In many libraries, the DDC is already online as a shelf list. An online shelf list is a very limited classified catalogue, but at least it permits users to browse at a terminal and is of some value to patrons and reference librarians in searching their collections. With the help of OCLC, Forest Press is hoping to study the possibilities of subject searching by Dewey numbers on an online public access catalogue. The data base anticipated by OCLC would return to the bibliographical (as opposed to the current exclusively bibliothecal) use of the DDC. If funds are granted, we anticipate a major project.

We find this project particularly exciting because if methodologies can be worked out, it will be possible to search not only local catalogues, but also regional and network data bases. Furthermore, the system may be used by any library, regardless of whether it uses the DDC to classify its own collections or not.

Elaine Svenonius in a recent article outlined various potential uses of classification in the online catalogue (noting some uses of the DDC). She is optimistic that classification (which has been theoretically moribund in the United States at least) will again become a topic of considerable interest.[5]

CONCLUSION

Reference librarians using the DDC are in a particularly good position to appreciate its advantages and limitations. The DDC is— as more than one librarian has pointed out—a "cognitive map" of a library's collection, providing a way to systematically think about the collection and to search it by subject. The territory being mapped out, however, is constantly being disturbed by minor changes in the configuration of the bibliographic landscape, and at times by major upheavals. The world mapped out by the 14th edition (to which many librarians look back with considerable nostalgia) is not recognizable today. Even the world mapped out by the 19th edition in 1979 has changed. Just as the reference librarian mediates between the user and this changing world of knowledge so too does the DDC. Therefore, the DDC must change.

The publisher and the Editor want the DDC to change in ways that will be most beneficial to all of its users, including reference librarians. Consequently, those involved in the preparation of the Dewey Decimal Classification encourage reactions from all of its users. If, in the past, the interests of users were not sufficiently taken into account, such is not the case today. Of all those involved with the DDC, no group is considered more important to those who produce the Classification than the librarians who use it. If it is not always possible to make requested changes, at least the rationale for decisions can be explained. Such requests constitute material for discussion by the Editorial Policy Committee when it advises the Editor and the Forest Press Committee.

For those who want to raise questions about the system, the following persons should be contacted:

1) With questions pertaining to general Dewey policy, and to publishing, production, and marketing matters for all Forest Press publications.

   John A. Humphry
   Executive Director
   Forest Press
   85 Watervliet Ave.
   Albany, NY 12206

2) With questions pertaining to the Classification, its application, development.

   Dr. John P. Comaromi
   Editor, DDC
   Decimal Classification Division
   The Library of Congress
   507 Madison Bldg.
   Washington, DC 20540

3) With questions pertaining to issues raised in the Annual Reports of the EPC (published in *LRTS* and *DC&*) and its meetings.

   Professor Margaret Cockshutt
   Chairperson, Editorial Policy Committee
   Faculty of Library and Information Science
   University of Toronto
   140 St. George St., Room 606
   Toronto, Ont., Canada M5S 1A1

4) With questions pertaining to the functions and activities of CCS and SAC as related to Dewey.	Lizbeth Bishoff, Head Librarian Ela Area Public Library Dist. 135 S. Buesching Rd. Lake Zurich, IL 60047

NOTES

1. Richard A. Gray, "Classification Schemes as Cognitive Maps," *The Reference Librarian*, No. 9, pp. 145-153.

2. See, for example, Sanford Berman, "DDC 19: An Indictment," *Library Journal* 105 (March 1980), 585-89; G. Bull and N. Roberts, review of *Dewey Decimal Classification and Relative Index*, 19th ed., *Journal of Librarianship* 12, no. 2 (April 1980), 139-42; Richard A. Gray, "Disasters: Natural, Nuclear, and Classificatory," *RQ* (Fall 1982): 42-47; see also various issues of *The Unabashed Librarian* and *Technicalities*.

3. Ingetraut Dahlberg, "Major Developments in Classification" in *Advances in Librarianship*, Vol 7, edited by Melvin J. Voigt and Michael H. Harris (New York: Academic Press, 1977), p. 68.

4. *Proposed Revision of 780 Music: Based on DEWEY Decimal Classification and Relative Index*, prepared under the direction of Russell Sweeney and John Clews, with assistance from Winton E. Matthews, Jr. (Forest Press, 1980), p. vii.

5. Elaine Svenonius, "Use of Classification in Online Retrieval," *Library Resources & Technical Services* (January/March 1983), pp. 76-80.

READERS' FORUM

Personality, Knowledge, and the Reference Librarian

Charles D. Patterson

In his thoughtful essay entitled "Some Unanswered Questions,"[1] Gerald Jahoda poses questions which have long perplexed many who are concerned about the reference function. The questions he raises have to do with 1) the desirable personality traits which one might expect the beginning reference librarian to possess and 2) the knowledge about reference work that junior reference librarians should have acquired and thus bring to the first position.

Of the first of these questions, concerning personality traits, Jahoda states: "Ideally, a reference librarian should have an outgoing personality, an ability to interact with all types of people, a logical and inquiring mind, and a strong desire to help people." Authors from Mudge to Hutchins to Katz have all addressed this subject and thus we are able to add to these, other important traits such as good memory, judgment, imagination, thoroughness, orderliness, persistency and accuracy, and the list goes on. However, this discussion will be limited to only those traits raised by Jahoda.

Here we are dealing with traits that are intangibles which, if they are innately imbued within the person, will, in all probability be developed, either partially or fully, by the time the student arrives at library school. These traits themselves are unteachable. However, if the individual has a spark of any of these traits it may be that situations can be created whereby they are developed through the ongoing activities of the reference and bibliography course. In order to

---

Charles D. Patterson is Professor, School of Library and Information Science, Louisiana State University, Baton Rouge, Louisiana.

achieve success in any reference course, ultimately much depends upon the skill and experience of the instructor. Of equal importance are the students whose personalities comprise the composition of any given class.

An outgoing personality is concomitant with the ability to successfully interact with all types of people. Certainly these are desirable traits which can be useful and effective in all human relations whether they are revealed at home, the workplace, or wherever. Being able to comfortably interact with others is fundamental to harmonious and worthwhile existence in any society and in all situations, in or out of the library. For those with these traits, smooth interactions flow quite naturally, while those without them will necessarily have to work very hard to develop these traits and the ability to utilize them effectively.

A logical and inquiring mind develops largely through self-discipline and study. This trait is among those which can be acquired in the classroom, laboratory, or outside any formal learning setting. One might reasonably expect that the student of librarianship (or any other profession or discipline) will have acquired and developed some inquisitiveness prior to entry in library school; although one can have an inquiring mind and lack any sort of logical sense, of any manner, concerning thought process. Without these, the person might be well advised to seriously consider employment alternatives other than reference librarianship.

Jahoda continues asking, "which of these traits are essential and which are merely nice to have?" Although each library school has its own admission standards and requirements, we are, nonetheless, left with what we can get. A small percentage of these people become reference librarians. Some students do exceptionally well, coming, as it were, into full bloom during the short period of time they are students. Others occupy space, barely emerge as personalities, and having departed, they continue to sit it out, regrettably, behind some reference desk. Which traits are essential and which are merely nice to have? As teachers it is our responsibility to nurture and encourage the development of those traits that are already within a person and which become evident throughout the duration of a course. One could hope that a few students will have some of these desirable traits, but unfortunately, none will have all of them. It becomes apparent that the "ideal" reference librarian is still standing in the wings, and we all eagerly await the appearance of this super person in the library world.

Jahoda continues stating that, "such traits are also needed for other, more prestigious and higher paying positions. Perhaps the implication in this statement is the administrative position; it is interpreted here as such. There is a long-standing and widely accepted fallacy that administration is the most difficult, most demanding and, therefore, the most deserving of the higher salary. This seems to be true in business, education, industry, and of course in the hierarchical structure of any larger library. In librarianship, we have only ourselves to blame for this prevalent misconception. The superior reference librarian should be rewarded and paid according to his or her effectiveness on the job; i.e., the reference desk and also in performing other assigned duties in the department. We continually hear of, read about and thus recognize the extreme importance of having access to information, the immediate availability of which is paramount in this technological age. In the library or information center, an essential key in locating information is the efficient and effective reference librarian. Unfortunately, salary schedules do not reflect these necessary but important intangible qualities which too few administrators acknowledge (or take for granted) as being essential in order to have quality service provided by the reference department. The work done by knowledgeable and experienced reference librarians is of equal importance to that done by the administrators and they should receive compensation that appropriately recognizes this very specialized expertise, even though the person may not be the department head. These points concerning the worth of the reference librarians can be made very effectively by instructors both in reference and management courses.

Attracting students to reference work depends upon the presence of many variables which involve the intelligence and enthusiasm of both the student and the instructor. The manner in which the reference class is conducted is very important. Sole reliance by the instructor upon the lecture method is neither desired nor ideal, and unless there is ample meaningful participation of every member of the class, the first step in favorably influencing students to seriously consider reference work will not be taken. The reference and bibliography course is a required or "core" course in most library education programs. Many students are in the course simply because they have to be, and these persons will, in all probability, never become reference librarians. However, there are students who, in the environment of an exceptional course and in the presence of a stimulating instructor, are positively motivated to change their minds about reference work. The seasoned instructor is usually able to identify those students who possess some of the desired traits and also those who demonstrate the potential for achieving success as reference librarians. These persons should be encouraged to the fullest and should enroll for additional reference and resource courses including independent studies which may center upon any of the many aspects of reference work. This important responsibility then rests with the instructor.

Jahoda's second question concerns the knowledge about reference that the student should possess. He queries, "Should students who will do reference work in libraries differing both in type and size have a working knowledge of context [content?] and organization of specific reference tools?" The answer here is an unequivocal "yes." Anything less, and we are severely selling short the prospective reference librarian. "Books remain basic, and a thorough knowledge of their content and arrangement is absolutely essential. This knowledge comes not just by their being talked about, but through direct experience with the books themselves; experience acquired both in and out of the classroom."[2] Because the basic reference course is mandatory for every student, it is difficult to tell, other than those few who demonstrate the enthusiasm and potential for this work during the course, just which students will continue on and become reference librarians. The point is, that if students are required, by the completion of the course, to actually demonstrate their knowledge of both arrangement and content of specific reference tools, their approach to any new or similar reference work will be largely affected in a positive way because of what was previously learned. Having become thoroughly acquainted with certain directories, bibliographies, indexes, etc., this familiarity is easily transferred to other reference works of the same type and format. This then is applicable in libraries differing both in type and size. For the student not planning on a reference career, exposure to this single course will at least provide some useful background should the need to function as a reference librarian ever arise.

In another aspect of this question Jahoda asks, "What should students know about the theory and the practice of the reference process?" There are many facets to this question, some of which are the administration and supervision of the reference department, bibliographic instruction, the appraisal function, and the reference interview, or interface. However, only the latter will be discussed here. Although the librarian may be thoroughly approachable and out-going, have an extensive knowledge of literally hundreds of sources (both within and outside the library) from which information may be drawn, it is a fact that unless this librarian also has total understanding of the fragile and extremely important process called the reference interview, nothing beneficial and useful to the patron will be accomplished. Fostering and developing the necessary skills involving voice modulation, body language and a sense of timing, etc., is an essential component of the reference and bibliography course. Providing opportunities for simulated situations, with all students participating, gives invaluable experience to the prospective reference librarian. Undoubtedly the emergence, understanding and proper utilization of these skills becomes evident more quickly in some students than in others. The art of adroitly asking appropriate questions to determine the precise needs of the patron is something that becomes better refined only through constant and extended practice. Depending upon the priorities previously established for the course by the instructor, greater or less time or emphasis may be allowed for meaningful experiences that strengthen the students' understanding of this fundamental part of reference work. Students then should know as much as possible about theory and practice of the reference process. It is in the reference interview, whether in person or by telephone, that all knowledge, skill, tact, imagination and ability to listen, come to bear.

A final question raised by Jahoda concerning communication skills with which the reference librarian should be equipped seems appropriate for closing this discussion. In order to have successful practice interviews in the course, as mentioned above, it is always highly desirable and very useful to have some students in the class whose first language is one other than English. The presence of these students provide excellent and realistic circumstances, and thus opportunities, for speaking, listening and comprehending, for both the student librarian and the student who assumes the role of the patron. In addition to identifying and correcting possible problems with language and communication, these situations also test the librarian's ability to think and react under pressure, as well as directly bringing to bear the student's accumulated knowledge of specific sources of information. These simulated reference situations augur well for the success of the beginning reference librarian.

As might be expected, this article closes with unanswered questions still unanswered, and we continue to search for those answers and solutions which enable us to better understand the reference function. However, in an area of librarianship which has been ploughed, worked, and reworked ad infinitum, perhaps a spadeful of fresh earth will have been overturned and thus provide opportunity for others to contribute to the ongoing discussions.

NOTES

1. Gerald Jahoda. "Some Unanswered Questions," *The Reference Librarian*, Numbers 1/2, Fall/Winter, 1981. p. 159.
2. Charles D. Patterson. "Books Remain Basic," *The Reference Librarian*, Numbers 1/2, Fall/Winter, 1981. pp. 171-172.

FORTHCOMING IN THE REFERENCE LIBRARIAN

LIBRARY INSTRUCTION AND REFERENCE SERVICES

Surveying of Instructional Needs Among Faculty and Students . . . John Lubans

Between the Mother Hen and Sink-or-Swim: Balancing Acts at the Reference Desk . . . . . John Swan

The Question of Questioning: The Reference Function and Continuing Instruction . . . . . John Budd

Bibliographic Education and Reference Service—A Continuum . . Mary Reichel

Training the Trainers: Inservice Methods for Reference Librarians Anne Roberts

Administrative Climate for B.I. in Research Libraries . . . . . Ron Blazek

Instruction and the Public Library . . . . . Estelle M. Black

Bibliographic Instruction and the Advancement of Reference Service . . . . . Kathy Coleman

Responsibility and Concerns for Administration of a Bibliographic Instruction Program in an Academic Library . . . . . Maureen Pastine

Library Instruction & Foreign Students: A Survey of Opinions and Practices Among Selected Libraries . . . . . Frank W. Goudy

Library Instruction through the Reference Query . . . . . Jane A. Reilly

Bibliographic Instruction or Reference? The Relationship Between Two Vital Public Services . . . . . Hannelore B. Radar

Toward Technical Services—Reference Cooperation in Library Instruction . . . . . Lois M. Pausch

Betwixt and Between: The Technical Services Librarian Involved In Reference and Instruction . . . . . Amy Dykeman

© 1984 by The Haworth Press, Inc. All rights reserved.

Metaphors and Mental Maps for Library Research Strategies . . . . Raymond G. McInnis
Library Instruction and the Reinforcement of Reference Service . . . C. Paul Vincent
The Complete Library Patron: An Essay on Fishing and Library Use . . . . . Robert Harris
Library Use Instruction with Individual Users: Instructional Techniques Applied to the Reference Interview . . . . . James Rice
Library Instruction: Are Principles from Adult Education Applicable . . . . . Patricia F. Beilke
Clues or Answers? Which Response to Library Users' Questions . . Ray Lester
Educating the Educators . . . . . Eric W. Johnson
No Royal Road . . . . . Melissa R. Watson
Is There a Librarian in the House . . . . . Debra J. Holland
Library Instruction in the Small/Medium Public Library: A Literature Survey . . . . . Jerry J. Carbone

EVALUATING REFERENCE SERVICES AND COLLECTIONS

Theory and Practice in the Collection and Analysis of Data Descriptive of Reference Desk Service . . . . . Margaret Joseph
Implementing the Evaluation Study . . . . . Sam Rothstein
Statistics and Evaluation . . . . . Juri and Jean Stratford
Evaluation of Methods of Evaluating Reference Services . . . . . Sydney Pierce
Evaluating the Reference Librarian . . . . . Bill Young
Why Not Accredit Reference Departments . . . . . Bernard Vavrek
Factors Affecting the Performance of Question Answering Services in Libraries . . . . . F. W. Lancaster
Reference Evaluation: What's the Use? . . . . . Eleanor J. Rodger
Evaluating Heavily Illustrated Reference Materials for Selection and Use . . . . . Charles Bunge
Tailoring Measures to Fit Your Service . . . . . Douglas L. Zweizig
Evaluation of Reference Services and Personnel . . . . . Terry L. Weech
Unobstrusive Evaluation of Reference Services—A One-Sided View of the Multifaceted Activity . . . . . Robert Harris
A Community Approach to Reference Evaluation in Public Libraries . . . . . Mary Lee Bundy

So What Do You Mean When You Say "A Good Reference Librarian" . . . . . Mignon Adams
Self-Diagnosis and Evaluation . . . . . Charles R. McClure
Definitions for Planning and Evaluating Reference Services . . . . . Katherine Emerson
The Whole Shebang—Comprehensive Evaluation of Reference Operations . . . . . Ellsworth Mason
Developing Criteria for Database Evaluation: The Example of Women's Studies . . . . . Sarah M. Pritchard
Qualitative Methods in the Evaluation of Reference Services . . . . . David Shavit
Use of Citation Studies in Evaluation . . . . . Alvin Schrader
Evaluating Bibliographic Instruction . . . . . Steve Falk

CONFLICTS IN REFERENCE SERVICES

Conflicts Between Interlibrary Loan and Reference Services . . . . . Marcia L. Sprules
Help/We Need a Better Name for What We Do . . . . . Paul Wiener
Conflict Between Libraries in Same Geographical Area . . . . . D. E. Davinson
Arbitrary Limits on the Public to Be Served . . . . . Peggy Sullivan
Conflicts Between Reference Librarians and Faculty Concerning Bibliographic Instruction . . . . . David Isaacson
Charging for Services: Then and Now . . . . . Margaret Steig
The Reference Librarian as Middleperson: Potential Conflicts Between Catalogers and Reference Librarians . . . . . Gillian M. McCombs
A Collection of Books: The College Professor vs the Reference Librarian . . . . . Melissa R. Watson
The Provision of Health Information to the Public . . . . . Robert Berk
The Role of the Reference Librarian as Viewed by Faculty and Administration in a College Library . . . . . Eric Johnson
Paying Twice: The Philosophy and Reality of Fees as a Barrier to Information Access . . . . . Dean Brugess
Between the Devil and the Deep Blue Sea-Reference: Some Conflicts and Dilemmas in Reference Service . . . . . George R. Bauer and Joan Robb
Role Ambiguity and Conflict in Reference Service: A Direction for Research . . . . . Henry R. Mendelsohn

Help Your Boss Support B.I. . . . . . Robert E. Brundin
The Encapsulated Reference Librarian: Breaking Down Departmental Barriers . . . . . Judith B. Quinlan
Reference Philosophy vs Service Reality . . . . . Larry D. Benson and Julene Butler
Yours, Mine or Ours: Identifying Who and How We Serve . . . . . Debbie Masters and Gail Flatness
The NASA Industrial Application Centers: Fee Based vs Free Information Services . . . . . Lynn Heer
Uneven Reference Desk Service . . . . . Fred Batt

For Product Safety Concerns and Information please contact our EU
representative GPSR@taylorandfrancis.com
Taylor & Francis Verlag GmbH, Kaufingerstraße 24, 80331 München, Germany

www.ingramcontent.com/pod-product-compliance
Lightning Source LLC
Chambersburg PA
CBHW052125300426
44116CB00010B/1784